THE
BEST
AMERICAN
POETRY
2002

◊ ◊ ◊

Robert Creeley, Editor

David Lehman, Series Editor

SCRIBNER POETRY

NEW YORK   LONDON   TORONTO   SYDNEY   SINGAPORE

SCRIBNER POETRY
1230 Avenue of the Americas
New York, NY 10020

SCRIBNER POETRY and design are trademarks
of Macmillan Library Reference USA, Inc., used under license
by Simon & Schuster, the publisher of this work.

For information regarding special discounts for bulk purchases,
please contact Simon & Schuster Special Sales at 1-800-456-6798
or business@simonandschuster.com

Manufactured in the United States of America

1   3   5   7   9   10   8   6   4   2

ISBN 0-7432-0385-2
0-7432-0386-0 (PBK)
ISSN 1040-5763

CONTENTS

David Lehman was born in New York City in 1948. He graduated from Columbia University in 1970, studied at Cambridge University in England as a Kellett Fellow, then returned to Columbia, where he was Lionel Trilling's research assistant. A Guggenheim Fellow, he is the author of five poetry books, including *The Daily Mirror: A Journal in Poetry* (2000) and *The Evening Sun* (2002), both from Scribner. Among his non-fiction books are *The Last Avant-Garde: The Making of the New York School of Poets* (Anchor, 1999) and *The Perfect Murder* (Michigan, 2000). With Star Black he is coeditor of *The KGB Bar Book of Poems* (Harper-Collins, 2000). He teaches writing and literature to graduate students at both the New School in New York City and Bennington College in Vermont, and offers a course on "Great Poems" in the undergraduate honors program at NYU. He is the general editor of the University of Michigan Press's Poets on Poetry Series. He initiated *The Best American Poetry* in 1988.

FOREWORD

by David Lehman

◊   ◊   ◊

The year 2001, like the year 1984 before it, arrived with heavy baggage. Both had existed (and do exist) outside of time as visions of tomorrow. Readers of George Orwell's *1984* may forever associate that eponymous year with the dystopian universe of Big Brother, the Thought Police, Newspeak, Hate Week, and Doublethink. Stanley Kubrick's 1968 movie *2001: A Space Odyssey* made the millennial turn seem synonymous with the sci-fi future, antiseptic but threatening, where spaceships dance to the *Blue Danube* and astronauts lose at chess to a sinister computer with a mind of his own. But where the actual 1984 came and went, a year vastly less memorable than Orwell's totalitarian prophecy ("a boot stamping on a human face—forever"), the year 2001 transcended the advance aura that Kubrick's amazing juxtapositions had produced.

The destruction of the World Trade Center and the massacre of the innocents was not only a catastrophic event in American history. It was also a revolutionary event in American consciousness. The day now marks a boundary: what was written, said, done, created before September 11 is seen as vitally different in kind and status from what since. It's as if history has returned to ground zero. The chalkboard has been wiped clean. But with the fresh start comes a new responsibility. Variants on Theodor Adorno's famous rhetorical question—How can there be poetry after Auschwitz?—were asked often against the backdrop of the blaze and rubble of downtown Manhattan. The spontaneous answer given by many was: How can there be not?

In their shock and grief, people everywhere looked instinctively to poetry. One poem more than any other was cited, recited, copied, e-mailed after the terrorist attacks on New York and Washington. W. H. Auden's "September 1, 1939" circulated electronically like one of the messages that "the Just / Exchange" in the form of "ironic points of light" (to borrow phrases from the poem's final stanza). Auden, a recent arrival in New York, wrote this ninety-nine-line poem on the day Germany invaded Poland and World War II commenced. The poem begins in "one of the dives / On Fifty-second Street" in Manhattan. Much of it seemed freshly apposite now: the "blind" skyscrapers in their verticality proclaiming the might of "Collective Man"; the commuters, addicted to their "habit-forming pain," occupying solitary stools in bars. The first stanza ends with lines that resonated eerily in the noxious air:

> The unmentionable odour of death
> Offends the September night.

Friends and strangers in chat rooms quoted this complex, difficult, ambiguous poem. So did sobersided CEOs. Newspapers coast to coast, from the *San Francisco Chronicle* to the *Baltimore Sun* and the *Boston Globe,* reprinted the entire poem on their editorial pages. It was e-mailed to me at least five or six times by, and I enjoyed the benefit of a correspondence with the poet and Williams College professor Lawrence Raab about the poem's rich but vexing penultimate stanza, which poets and critics have argued about for years:

> All I have is a voice
> To undo the folded lie,
> The romantic lie in the brain
> Of the sensual man-in-the-street
> And the lie of Authority
> Whose buildings grope the sky:
> There is no such thing as the State
> And no one exists alone;
> Hunger allows no choice
> To the citizen or the police;
> We must love one another or die.

Was one example of the "folded lie" a newspaper? Did the colon after "sky" imply that the lines that follow are types of lies? The most vexing question had to do with the stirring last line. Was it mendacious to the precise extent of its rhetorical effectiveness? In what sense can love prevent or save us from death? Of what use was such a declaration—or was it a piety—in the face of Nazi military aggression? (As Maggie Nelson wrote in a different context, "you can't hug / a Nazi and hope / he'll change.") Auden, who took self-criticism seriously, so despised the stanza's final line (for some the poem's best) that he changed it to the unsatisfactory "We must love one another and die," and later decided to disown the poem altogether. "It may be a good poem, but I shouldn't have written it," he maddeningly said.

The wild popularity of "September 1, 1939" was that rare thing, a phenomenon that had erupted on its own without orchestration or hype. The poem's apparent ubiquitousness was analyzed almost as much as the poem itself. "It is the poem for our present pain," Eric McHenry wrote in *Slate,* in part because it seems "weirdly prescient" and in part because of its mood of doubt. Sven Birkerts in the *New York Observer* called it Auden's "most sustaining" poem, an example of poetry as "the reverse of the terrorist act." I would add that Auden's poems—not only the one in question but such others as the elegies for Yeats and Freud, "Caliban to the Audience" and "In Praise of Limestone"—attract readers who value the poetry of civilized discourse and believe in the power (and the limits) of human reason. For Dana Gioia in *The Dark Horse,* the immediate resort to "September 1, 1939" helped make the case for poetry's civic, public, and ceremonial uses. It reinforced, in his view, the priority of "expressive power" over "stylistic novelty" as a poetic virtue. On the other hand, Daniel Swift, reporting on the American scene for the London *Times Literary Supplement,* was not alone in recoiling from the "trace of something almost nasty in this poem," either a whiff of self-congratulation (Swift) or evidence of "incurable dishonesty" (Auden). Unsurprisingly there was as little agreement on the cultural meaning of the phenomenon as on Auden's unorthodox use of colons and unusual adjectives ("clever hopes," "the conservative dark") within the poem itself, thus demonstrating that poetry as an essence precedes and supersedes the contestation of meanings and interpretations to which it gives rise.

"September 1, 1939" was not the only poem to hit the bulletin boards. On *Slate* Robert Pinsky recommended Marianne Moore's "What Are Years?" as well as poems by Edwin Arlington Robinson, Czeslaw Milosz, and Carlos Drummond de Andrade. Alicia Ostriker on the MobyLives Web site picked the same sublime Moore poem plus works by Yehuda Amichai, Stephen Dunn, and Hayden Carruth. The hunger for poetry and the need for elegy resulted in impromptu or hastily arranged public readings with overflow audiences. On an October evening, more than a thousand people crowded into the Great Hall of Cooper Union in New York to listen to poems "in a time of crisis." Newspapers ran numerous articles on poetry's power to heal and console. Anthologies comprising "responses" to September 11 or poems from "post–9/11 New York" were planned. For the poets themselves, all this attention was not an unmixed blessing: the pressure to write poetry equal to an occasion can sometimes lead to an outpouring of mediocre verse. A bad poem is no less bad for the nobility of the sentiments expressed. "You can't approach something like this frontally in a poem—at least I can't," Billy Collins told a reporter. "It will knock you over. It is like walking into a big wave. You will fall on your bathing suit." Collins clarified his position in *USA Today*. "It's not that poets should feel a responsibility to write about this calamity," he wrote. "All poetry stands in opposition to it. Pick a poem, any poem, from an anthology and you will see that it is speaking for life and therefore against the taking of it. A poem about mushrooms or about a walk with the dog is a more eloquent response to September 11 than a poem that announces that wholesale murder is a bad thing."

No stranger to this anthology series—his work was chosen by guest editors Charles Simic, Louise Glück, James Tate, John Hollander, Robert Bly, Rita Dove, and Robert Hass—Collins was tapped in June to succeed Stanley Kunitz as the nation's poet laureate. "We should notice that there is no prose laureate," Collins said at the news conference, "although they will probably be lobbying for equal treatment." The new laureate's populist appeal is beyond dispute. You can coerce people to do many things, but buying books of poetry isn't one of them, and people buy Collins's books in quantity. He has real readers, readers who aren't themselves poets, who obey the pleasure principle when it comes to buying a book. But the *New York Times* in a front-page story anointed him as "the most popular poet in America" and he has since become a magnet for envy. In an application of what I've come to call the Resentment Index, I realized that Collins had truly made it when I began hearing his work disparaged regularly. The Fall 2001 issue of the *Melic Review* contained no fewer than four poems satirizing the poet's geniality and embrace of the quotidian. (One dastardly fellow's parody would, however, "direct you to that lampshade / made of human skin and tell you / to concentrate on the warm glow // and forget the camps." Even bad taste should have its bounds.) Collins's poetry was too easy for the *New Republic*'s Adam Kirsch, who complained: "Nothing in his work suggests that he even acknowledges that there is a place for difficulty in poetry. His amused indifference resembles wisdom only as death resembles life." Of course, nothing in Collins's work denies a place for difficulty in poetry, or implies even remotely that he aims to dictate what other poets do, but that's not the point. The inflated simile ("as death resembles life") suggests the vehemence of the critical antagonism that a poet of humor and warmth, ease of manner, and above all a large audience can expect. Well, critics will be critics, though the public at any rate clearly counts neither Auden's difficulty nor Collins's accessibility as strikes against them.

Adoring fans weighed in elsewhere. The magazine *Whetstone* published an unconventional marriage proposal in the form of Lisa Beyer's poem "Billy Collins's Wife," the title indicating what she, author or speaker, would yearn to be if there were a vacancy. ("For this to be so / Billy Collins's wife / must die a death / both quick and painless, / but especially quick, / so I will still be 32 / and possessing whatever / loveliness I ever possessed, / for what else can I offer such a man?") As the war against the Taliban and al-Qaeda heated up, the novelist Ira Levin suggested that our poet laureate ("what's he there for?") be asked to propose code names superior to the widely deplored monikers Operation Infinite Justice and Operation Enduring Freedom. Collins soon disclosed "Poetry 180," his own sensible idea for how best to use his office. He crafted a list of 180 poems, one for each school day, in an initiative to get poetry read aloud daily in high schools.

It was poetry as usual for much of 2001, "usual" in this case signifying its opposite, and "poetry" here referring to anything that claims to be such. There were reminders that April, National Poetry Month, begins with a day that honors the fool. In Alaska, the arts council launched a poetry initiative that prompted the Borealis Brewery to print poems on beer bottles. A more dubious second result was that 250,000 Alaskans, or 40 percent of the state's population, opened their telephone, water, and sewer bills in April and found a poem stuffed inside as filler. (It was Tom Sexton's "Beluga," about the white whales that swim Cook Inlet off Anchorage each June.) Later in the year, Oprah Winfrey demonstrated that her awesome marketing muscle applies as well to poetry as to fiction. When she praised the poems of Mattie Stepanek, an eleven-year-old boy who suffers from muscular dystrophy, she did so rhapsodically, with a tear in her eye. "If ever I had a book to recommend, it's Mattie's. If ever you were going to buy a book, I recommend it; this is the one, my friends." (Mattie had previously stolen the show at the Jerry Lewis Labor Day telethon.) *Journey Through Heartsongs* promptly sold 170,000 copies, and a second Stepanek book soon joined it on the bestseller list. An anthology of Jacqueline Kennedy Onassis's *Best-Loved Poems,* also a best-seller, included several of Jackie's youthful efforts in verse, which did nothing to diminish her iconic status.

On June 11, Timothy McVeigh, facing execution for his part in the Oklahoma City bombing of 1995, chose to make no personal statement but instead referred the media to W. E. Henley's "Invictus," a nineteenth-century warhorse that schoolchildren used to have to memorize. "My head is bloody, but unbowed," wrote Henley, who suffered from tuberculosis and had to have a leg amputated. The poem concludes: "I am the master of my fate; / I am the captain of my soul." I went on a local New York TV newscast to infer that McVeigh remained unrepentant. In the green room before going on the air I could see the monitor and how I was billed. No name; it just said "execution poem expert." Meanwhile a *New York Times* reporter asked poets and critics which poem they would choose to help them "embrace the moment" if they "knew the hour of their death in advance." The seventeenth-century poet George Herbert won. Molly Peacock, Robert Pinsky, and Helen Vendler all picked a Herbert poem, though Dana Gioia held out for Tennyson's "In Memoriam" and Richard Howard for Wallace Stevens's "Sunday Morning."

Since its inception as an annual anthology in 1988, *The Best American Poetry* has acted on the notion that the best way to honor excellence in poetry is to enlist a poet of distinguished stature to do the choosing each year. By this means each volume in the series necessarily differs from its predecessor, and the books taken together chronicle the taste of some of our leading poets. Robert Creeley, this year's editor, is esteemed among fellow poets across the board irrespective of affiliation and orientation. Donald Hall, who made the selections for *The Best American Poetry 1989*, once said that the poet of his generation he admires most is Creeley: "I love his marching ear and the delicacy of his nuances." Like others I first fell under Creeley's spell when I read Donald M. Allen's *New American Poetry* in the 1960s. His poems had an easy intimacy; they advanced their propositions tersely and without pomp ("If you never do anything for anyone else / you are spared the tragedy of human relation- // ships"). Creeley is universally admired for his skill at line breaks. Trying to explain his magic, I wrote: "it / doesn't matter / what he says / what matters is / the way the lines / break at just / the right moment / each time / uncanny." Few editors in my experience have been as decisive and confident as Creeley. It was, as I could have predicted, a pleasure to work with him.

Clever former English majors continue their subversive campaign to insinuate poetry into popular culture, sometimes to brilliant or hilarious effect. In the movie *The Anniversary Party,* Kevin Kline, playing an actor, quotes the conclusion of Matthew Arnold's "Dover Beach" ("Ah, love, let us be true to one another . . .") as a toast to the reconciling Hollywood couple whose anniversary it is. It is solemn, deadpan, and completely inappropriate—quite as if the movie had taken to heart Anthony Hecht's parody of Arnold ("The Dover Bitch") and realized how odd it must feel to be "addressed / As sort of a mournful cosmic last resort." Poetry is a great prophetic warning of "ignorant armies" on contested beachheads, but it is also the lampooning of that impulse. And it is passion, or an adolescent's intense longing for it: the plot of the French thriller *With a Friend Like Harry* hinges on a poem the hero wrote for his *lycée* literary magazine, which his curious "friend" still knows by heart though many years have elapsed.

Poetry, the art of articulation, renders us inarticulate when it comes to defining it. Purists would discourage us from considering poetry as an essence, or as anything apart from individual texts, but there remains the obdurate attachment to poetry as not only an art but a quality in itself that a person or a work of art may have. "I'm not just a suit," said Gerald Levin when he retired as CEO of AOL Time Warner last December. "I want the poetry back in my life." Similarly, Woody Allen, accounting for his preference in movie westerns, said, "*Shane* achieves a certain poetry that *High Noon* doesn't." It is tempting to conclude that poetry remains the touchstone art, a supreme signifier, emblematic of soulful artistry, the adventurous imagination, and the creative spirit.

Robert Creeley was born in Arlington, Massachusetts, in 1926. He describes himself as a New Englander by birth and disposition, although he has spent much of his life in other parts of the world, including Guatemala, British Columbia, France, and Spain. In 1954 Charles Olson invited him to teach at Black Mountain College, where Creeley founded and edited *The Black Mountain Review*. He taught at the University of New Mexico and the University of British Columbia and in 1966 began teaching at the State University of New York in Buffalo, where in time he was made the Samuel P. Capen Professor of Poetry and the Humanities. He was cofounder of the Poetics Program there (1991) and its first director. With the exception of *Life & Death* (New Directions, 1998) his poems are now collected in three volumes—*Collected Poems, 1945–1975* (University of California Press, 1982), *So There: Poems 1976–83* (New Directions, 1998), and *Just in Time: Poems 1984–1994* (New Directions, 2001). He has also published a novel and a collection of stories, which have recently been reissued with other prose works in *Collected Prose* (Dalkey Archive Press, 2001). In 1999 a traveling exhibition of Creeley's work with such artists as Jim Dine, R. B. Kitaj, Alex Katz, John Chamberlain, Francesco Clemente, and Susan Rothenberg (*In Company: Robert Creeley's Collaborations*) was shown at the New York Public Library and at other venues across the country. He won the Bollingen Prize in 1999, the Before Columbus Foundation's Lifetime Achievement Award in 2000, and the Lannan Foundation's Lifetime Achievement Award in 2001. When not in Buffalo, New York, he lives in Waldoboro, Maine.

INTRODUCTION

by Robert Creeley

◇   ◇   ◇

My sister, Helen Power, died early this January. She had been ill for some real time with rheumatoid arthritis and a number of other things coincident. She was four years older than I, seventy-nine, and had certainly lived a full and varied life, as one says. She was my instruction for such things as this book makes clear—poetry, feelings, the common world we live in, and what one cares about and what one doesn't. While still a teenager she won a prize in a contest judged by Robert P. Tristram Coffin, the Maine poet, for a poem she or perhaps her teacher had submitted. It's very hard for me to think I'd even be in this situation now, much less a poet, were it not for the precedent and means she both directed me to and, in a way, insisted upon.

Whether or not there is finally the "best" of anything is no doubt a moot point. Yet one wants for those here assembled not only Coleridge's "willing suspension of disbelief," which enables all and any reality to be the case, but also a recognition that they are those who, as Charles Olson wrote on his own behalf, "live [their] lives quite properly in print." It's not that they don't each one have other lives, of whatever significance or value. But here they are as these words, and structures of words, allow them to be, neither more nor less.

That fact, then, will have to do with how any one of us will find them. I cannot tell you sufficiently how frustrating the job was of going through countless journals, online as well as off, of trying so to find for myself enough, to feel at least I'd been open, been fair, to the occasion. Of course, that itself is only wishful thinking. Poetry may have an apparently objective presence—this word saying that, this line having this length and number. But, as Louis Zukofsky aptly wrote, one might spend a lifetime trying to differentiate between the articles "a" and "the"—an instance is never quite the same as the thing itself.

So, of course, it turns out that "Beauty is in the eye of the beholder . . ." just as it always was. *You think that's the best way to put it? I don't*—or *do,* as the case may be. As I read through the myriad poems that were to be considered, I had to wonder if poetry, whatever it is, was meant to be a *multiple,* call it—a mass, like a flock of geese going south for the winter or an early-morning traffic jam. Did people read poems the way they might read newspapers, or books on a subject, or weather forecasts? Did more of them mean more information of whatever kind they seemed to provide?

When I was young, it was Ezra Pound who most equipped me with rules of thumb for thinking about poetry, and also for trying to make it. He advised the aspirant to listen to the sound that it makes and felt that poetry atrophied when it got too far from music. One should not forget that poets are literally "makers," and that, recalling W. C. Williams's preface to *The Wedge* (1944), "A poem is a small (or large) machine made of words." It is also useful to think of what Christopher Small proposes in his book *Musicking: The Meanings of Performing and Listening* (1998), to wit, that music is not a product, a thing one can conclude and package. It is primarily an *activity,* something happening—which then relates to the art world's preoccupation with "happenings" of some years ago, that yearning to break free of the didactic box of fixed measures and expectations. So, too, poetry may well be "going on," whether in the person of the reader or the poet—just as for Keats:

> Forlorn! the very word is like a bell
> To toll me back from thee to my sole self!
> Adieu! the fancy cannot cheat so well
> As she is fam'd to do, deceiving elf.
> Adieu! adieu! thy plaintive anthem fades
> Past the near meadows, over the still stream,
> Up the hill-side; and now 'tis buried deep
> In the next valley-glades:
> Was it a vision, or a waking dream?
> Fled is that music:—Do I wake or sleep?

It happens and it is, as Keats says, often a "music."

My grandmother could recite poems endlessly. A practical, working-class woman from Maine, she had a store of poems she much valued. Our mother was named after the heroine in the Bangor newspaper's serial novel of that moment, *Genevieve.* In any case, our grandmother loved that other world. As my sister wrote, "I still can hear her in the pantry, rolling out dough and reciting for her own pleasure—so many poems . . ."

> Fair Charlotte lived by the mountainside
> In a wild and lonely spot—
> No house there was for five miles around
> Except her father's cot. . . .

A poet happily here included told me that his interest in Louis Zukofsky was once questioned by his then instructor and fellow poet, who said, "How can you possibly value a poet who is not only hard to understand but whose poems themselves are impossible ever to remember?" Whereupon the first poet began quoting from Zukofsky's "A" until the other finally begged for mercy. "What thou lov'st well shall not be reft from thee . . ." Neither book nor blanket nor mind—it's yours, presuming you hold on to it. Asked by my sister why it was she so cared for poems, our grandmother answered that she liked to have something in her head.

So what is *best* then? How is that choice ever to be made? Despite all the accumulating opinions, or, as it is called, criticism, how can one possibly claim to know what's best in any respect? I think of the debris of such assertion over the years I've lived. Was World War II the best? Was "Better Living Through Chemistry" the best chance we all had? Or, even more haunting, *Is this the best we can do?*

I'd like therefore to dismiss that specious and insupportable claim, at least for this present volume. These poems are *better* than the best, each and every one of them. If you don't agree, then go find your own—which is not offered as a challenge. Rather as fact of what, one has to recognize, is the point of any of this to begin with, that we are "instructed, moved and delighted" by poetry, as Pound said, quoting Agricola, who had said it centuries before him. Just as poetry has finally no school sufficient for the learning of its art, no persons more than "called," Wordsworth writes, from which number "few are chosen," what one can use as measure and judgment has finally to do with his or her own perceptions and needs in that complex of others with whom one shares a life. Insofar as we are human, I presume we all will have some term in common. But it is not a didactic frame, a perversely Procrustean "bed," wherewith to confound all that will not, or that refuses to, "fit."

Quite the contrary. The pleasure of these poems is, first of all, that they caught my fancy, some almost outrageously, some by their quiet, nearly diffident manner, some by unexpected turns of thought or insight, others by a confident authority and intent. There could be no rule that would necessarily include them all as a company here. I think of Robert Duncan's saying, "I can't remember if I wrote it or I read it!" It was that kind of closeness, as if I'd come into an unexpected clearing, a space I had not known was there, and in it was something equally both familiar and strange, something *new* to me, that freshened ways I took the world and myself to be existing, and also made me at home in it. Just as my grandmother did, I wanted something in my head, I wanted the literal comfort of words, I wanted them to tell me things, all things, anything. I wanted them to speak to me.

When I was a young man, I showed chickens at the Boston Poultry Show, a regal event that used to take place on Huntington Avenue in the old Mechanics Hall. All one could see looking in were myriad tiers of cages, all with chickens in them, all colors, sizes, featherings, even skins—some were a curious purplish color, for example. Some were designated "Polish," "Chinese," even "Rhode Island (Reds)." They had come from everywhere. Mine were Dark Brahmas. I had a few Barred Plymouth Rocks and Silver-Laced Wyandottes, but the Dark Brahmas were my particular hope and care. If you know about chickens, you will know there is a *Standard of Perfection,* which is a detailing of the requisite confirmation, color, feather, feet, wattle, leg, and so forth. Whatever can be thought of as the physical constitution of a chicken is specified and described. No one really wants now to consider that the word "chicken" itself relates to the male sex, *cock,* much as one might suspect. No one wishing to make something simply stay put will want it to go on changing by any such process as life and death. "Poultry," on the other hand, means chickens in quite another guise, a *poule*—which curiously comes from the feminine of *pullus,* "a young animal"—and has lent itself to other uses expectably unapproved. Poultry? "I too dislike it."

So one took care, read the *Standard,* observed the birds, bred them to their genetic strengths until it came to pass that one could lay a pencil across the dark barring on a Barred Rock's flight feather and see only white either side. Just so one might ruffle the breast or thigh fluff and find no trace of smut, no tinge of darkened feathers. My mother, when still a child, lacking dolls, would dress their chickens in the garments our grandmother had made for the one doll she did have, little dresses and coats she managed to pull onto them, wings sticking out through the little arm holes. I used to take our chickens, tuck their heads under their wings, then holding them in a sort of sling fashion, rock them back and forth for a few minutes until I could lay them almost anywhere on their sides. There they would stay, in a sort of trance. We thought of them as "hypnotized."

There's something Pound says somewhere, which argues that the experience of beauty comes from one's recognition of a thing's perfections, *how* it is what it is, not necessarily why. *Why* peculiarly invites a judgment which has most to do with one's own terms of understanding. In the poem, however, that place we are finally safe in, understanding is not a requirement. You don't have to know why. Being there is the one requirement.

It was Williams's contention that "a new world is only a new mind" and that "the mind and the poem are all apiece." Charles Olson felt that "art [was] the only true twin life has." Either would seem to emphasize that our human ways of apprehending the world, what we can recognize thus as being the world, is a fact of our imagining it, an act of figuring, of making a picture for ourselves of what it seems to be. Culturally, complexly, we are given such a picture at birth, an *imago mundi,* and no doubt our transformations and reconfigurings of that represented place are finally quite small in their effect. Even what happens takes a long time to happen, not before but after the event. It's as if we were living so far off in our various spaces that sounds came first a long way to find us and then took an equal time to be heard and taken in. Poetry asks first that one bear witness, that one come in, that one willingly suspend disbelief. Only the habits and demands of a usual religion are perhaps more particular in this way. But religion has an end in view. Unlike poetry, it would think to know where it was going before it had ever got there. There are so many ways we are, each so curiously familiar. There is so much to be said, first for the first time, and then over and over and over.

What was I doing, or thinking to provide for, taking a copy of Pound's *A Draft of XXX Cantos* into the Second World War? I had thought I was to join the American Field Service unit in Italy but found myself in India instead, and then Burma. I wrote V-Mail letters to my sister and mother. What could be "best" in that confused time and who could possibly know what any of us were doing?

> Kung walked
> > by the dynastic temple
> and out into the cedar grove,
> > and then out by the lower river,

And with him Khieu, Tchi
       And Tian the low speaking
And "we are unknown," said Kung,
"You will take up charioteering?
     "Then you will become known,
"Or perhaps I should take up charioteering, or archery?
"Or the practice of public speaking?"
And Tsieru-lou said, "I would put the defences in better order,"

And Khieu said, "If I were lord of a province
"I would put it in better order than this is."
And Tchi said, "I would prefer a small mountain temple,
"With order in the observances,
     with a suitable performance of the ritual,"
And Tian said, with his hand on the string of his lute,
The low sounds continuing
     after his hand left the strings,
And the sound went up like smoke, under the leaves,
And he looked after the sound:
     "The old swimming hole,
"And the boys flopping off the planks,
"Or sitting in the underbrush playing mandolins."
     And Kung smiled upon all of them equally.
And Thseng-sie desired to know:
     "Which had answered correctly?"
And Kung said, "They have all answered correctly,
"That is to say, each in his nature."

                    (from *Canto XIII*)

I thought that these poems now to follow were the best among a great many that might well follow them and also be the best, and that they in turn might well find others, so that they also might follow, and be the best, too—for each time, each place, and each person.

THE
BEST
AMERICAN
POETRY
2002

◇ ◇ ◇

Up to Speed

◇ ◇ ◇

Streamline to instantaneous
voucher in / voucher out
system.

The plot winnows.

The Sphinx
wants me to guess.

Does a road
run its whole length
at once?

Does a creature
curve to meet
itself?

Whirlette!

★

Covered or cupboard
breast? Real

housekeeping's
kinesthesiac. Cans

held high
to counterbalance "won't."

★

Is it
such agendas

which survive
as souls?

★

Vagueness is personal!

A wall of concrete bricks,
right here,
while sun surveys its grooves

and I try
"instantly" then "forever."

But the word is
way back,
show-boating.

Light is "with God"

(light, the traveler).

★

Are you the come-on
and the egress?

One who hobbles by
determinedly?

Not yet?

from *Chicago Review*

JOHN ASHBERY

The Pearl Fishers

◊   ◊   ◊

And he would say, "You ought to write him and thank him for it,"
    and I'd
say, "Yes, I'm going to when I have the time." Of course I had intended
to, but the project aged. It was slightly too dry. I'll begin again, I'll
thank him. And so I did, in my own way. I forgot him and his seven
    journeys
to success. We became as one—a stilt. A single stilt isn't of much use,
and that's how I thanked him—by reminding him from time to time,
as the salt ball rolled toward the glacier.

It melted and did not. Wait, you can't get up. There's A1 sauce

on her slipcover. Informality be damned, he said. Whenever I come here I
like to take two lumps instead of three. Unfortunately you can't have
    either,
we're out of everything I said. The sun smiled wanly on the Cimmerian
    landscape,
which stirred. It seemed as if it was at last about to take an interest

in rubber goods,
piles of filth,
gossamer undies,
potted hyacinths,
stumps no tree would own up to,
casinos rattling till three in the morning.

I'm sorry, Mrs. Swan-toe,
we meant not to disturb and then this waterfall

rushed over the island, as I'm sure you noticed. By the time it had
      passed
fully, except for the occasional unavoidable runnel,
no one could remember how to count.

It was a Royal Accident.
You can't rely on those,
they always win.

                              from *Verse*

The Golgotha Local

◇　◇　◇

Then the question rose,
How would you sustain consciousness?
In the madness of the eat shit world / (How would you,
　　How would you . . . It became a song)
Now I don't want to whine and whimper, this is the old and
　　the new
Where you come in I was too and left to go left and to come right in
There is no one you know closer than you know me except me
　　knowing you

You was there? You felt the stare of the streets, the wind
Screaming you submit to these motherfuckers
You ain't shit / I was in the under world of thought
Where yesterday bounces off what it know and
Descends to your shoetops as scraps of NO
You ain't even gon pick up. I'll pick up a brown
Ass penny, I know that story, how they got us
In purgatory. The civil war, the south, the journey
To yesterday, I know all that, I use it, or get my hat . . . Get to That.

But if you understood, the entire question, the pause, the certain
　　ugliness
Of what you see, if between they legs you got to look, if you is
　　ruled by thief and
crook. If you is more than what you be, and you is not the you
we see. Look, is that you. Look, listen, feel, when I walk at night
And see your children, mine is with them, and then the heathen
Come and whip them, instruct them in our knees give them souls
　　made of pleas.

Then what
If Angry dumb   you be they   belly
babbling we know

Paradise, will is you really playing crap
& none a us ain't got no dice
Is song a thug funk more mariney was dig
Behind we cannot see   is be   our map,   who mouth
a trap
What is there to
Say or do. Where are the what is really you? Who is them what
    say you them
Why you so smart and always lose. Who is the image in your
    mirror?
If you ain't sure. But don't be starin, get so out you lie for carin
Ok Ok Ok
OK OK OK

Just one minute, before you blank, the shit gone stay, the shit
    that stank, that shit
Gon stay, and you gon lay, and what you is is drove away.
    OK OK OK
Ask Miles Davis, he dead, So What?

                    from *Skanky Possum*

12²

◇ ◇ ◇

the swollen flotsam
lies face down
accordingly

---

incident catches
stolen cues
when faces drift

---

encroachment of care
muffling shame
hardened moment

---

like flies in summer
switching tenses
touched absence

totally wasted
in shadows
imperceptible

---

uncertain future
annoying
complacency

---

neither this nor that
bombs away
total fright

---

unendurable
even if it
will also pass

---

my elbow against your
composure
burns like wax

incapacity
telescopes
endlessly fog

counting now to five
next to three
then up till four

going back to form
a promise
always broken

from *Slope*

from Zero Star Hotel

◇   ◇   ◇

At the Smith and Jones
Factory I get my
Gear, don't smoke
Don't vote, dry off
With Madonna towel
It's a field night
For the roachies
Smoked too many
Crumbs, too much
Genre manipulation

looks like nothing
ever happened
except everything's
wet, singed cork
rubbeth face, pay
concierge/owner
in red-checked pjs
for Ross' 8 nights decapitate
writer head and sacrifice
to gods of buried vocals

DugRoth says id Keats
Was here in our burgers
He'd slug him every time
If he played the Welt-
Meister? Double
Slug. West Nile Virus
Strikes Bill Five Times
Tho' he's scared to enter
Queens, despite status
As honorary Met

Metro musician speaks:
"If the global workforce
continues to be decimated
by disease & natural catas-
trophe it will be necessary
to clone a workforce.
please give in advance
to help create this force
in exchange for these
accordion songs. Merci."

It takes a dick
To raise a pyramid
Motorcycle crash
On the tongue, small
Business buried, this short
But expansive demonological
Expose is, in all probability
My own diabolized & garbled
Version of raising "the listener"
To the rank of dualist "believer"

The moral right of the author
Has been deserted
And tearful words that rhyme
You are not crumbling and
You are tired of crumbling
The moral continuum
Of the gobot's heresy
Has been dejected
With feelings of paranoia
Thank Augustine, for

Many otters are also
Making current loans
Whilst unable
To find the function
Button next to the
Pause button.
While you were invisible
I was privvy
To the seamscape
Brutish preconfiguring was there

three nines, plus fifteen
two fours king high, lose five
two fives ace high, lose five
nothing ace high, lose finger
right index. Zilch, ace
high, lose left thumb
ten and seven pairs, get thumb
back, doesn't fit. Two fives
hand back thumb. Six high
lose hand, split.

like Leonard Nimoy
you and I are made
mostly of water. But
when the assholes play
ukeleles and gloat
about cheap rent
the sight of the world
quarters me. Thus I regress
shame and embarrassment
fucking up the life

end poem with gambling
write out dreams
another personal rule
broken to quote face
death unquote, with
apologies to the just now
stomped roachie.
"they were all my friends
and they died," an old
thread and a new one

Coptic art, blue lady
Bahrain coin, midnight
Medoc, Eddie snickers
Insects attack, denim guy
Who robs drug stores
Yearning to speak:
Cocktail fugitive angst
Ball refuses to be thrown
Be not frozen in cigar
Store scared to emote

basically we need
a cultural tilting of the bowl
or diseased markets. Interrogation
chairs pile up outside
guides. Primitives drool
intelligence. I can't find
the light. Two degrees
outside. The city at odds.
poetry is my strength
clothes are my weakness

Nobody comes over
And never leaves anymore
Incidental back to a sill
Calm, poignant and terrified
Volunteer me a busride
Chase middle fingers with bats
Blooming by the pond
I did not hug the tranquil
Endowment after a wedding
Drank everything I could

pigeon now weird big
books everywhere jogging
in hollywood t-shirts
we raised this park
and built a pond by
which to shoot movies
they shot us on the pond
and it was the best I hate
that dog I ever had
feeding with a bottle

Now Eddie's bored
People invented God
To excuse their bad
Habits this roach
Says to me. There
Isn't anyone it
Even wants to imitate
Eddie and I play anti-
Chess, both begin
In check

now Ross is gone
bearer of sock herb
impresser of exiled
temps. Um is my
comment, leaking
uranium on the sea
bed. Others tilt
ever so slightly
swoopward, blame
the spiritual outsider

At the reading reaching
For the bar food "Well
We've got to put those
Subs somewhere or else
Sell them as staples
Of a fast food fat
Reducing diet. Find
And replace he said
I see a crabby
Peering through a crag

I've never met any
Mysterious musicians
Sorry. I wish
They stopped saying
Lord, and ended
This Pope business
My relative Clapp
Died at the Alamo
Let's give Texas
Back to Mexico

Solid boundless freefall
My connective tissue
My fine citizen centering
Circles this frame
Upside down flying
Back first into
Woods, flipped
Over handlebars
Brake cord detached
Leaf imprint on back

passenger next to antagonist
all my darkness is product
I sell it your way as wisdom
you lose blue, use red
I see my feet sometimes
artificial's the right word
clinical joy unreported
poke a hole in a blanket
and with your head
go through it

the original of this
poem is available
for $5,000. When
I sell it I plan
to buy a debris
slide. I'm broke
but I make more
money than my
parents did when
they were my age

what is interesting
about him is also what
is wrong with him
rendering him electable
he's the guy who poses
for trophies, biologically
but he is turning into
bio-seitan, to be eaten
by a despicably healthy
human extending a lifespan

I can get a sparrow
With a bow and arrow
I can buy anything
Cheaper than you
Who wasted the miracle
On the dove?
The subject is SAME
NAME. There's nothing
To cross out. $5,000!
Have a happy warning

if you don't understand
don't be ashamed
to ask three times
the answer is TIGHT-LIPPED
you have won $30,300
can I have a glass of water?
the Americans had Judy
Garland & we had Edie Piaf
he was set to do another season
of Superman, then he was shot

from *Bombay Gin*

FRANK BIDART

Injunction

◇ ◇ ◇

As if the names we use to name the uses of buildings
x-ray our souls, war without end:

Palace. Prison. Temple. School.
Market. Theater. Brothel. Bank.

War without end. Because to name is to possess
the dreams of strangers, the temple

is offended by, demands the abolition of brothel, now theater, now
school; the school despises temple, palace, market, bank; the bank by

refusing to name depositors welcomes all, though in rage prisoners each
night gnaw to dust another stone piling under the palace.

War without end. Therefore time past time:

Rip through the fabric. Nail it. Not
to the wall. Rip through

the wall. Outside

time. Nail it.

from *Ploughshares*

15

The Body

◊　◊　◊

---

1 It was the particular feel of him that made me want to go back: everything that is said is said underneath, where, if it does matter, to acknowledge it is to let on to your embarrassment. That I love you makes me want to run and hide.

2 It is not the story I know or the story that you tell me that matters; it is what I already know, what I don't want to hear you say. Let it exist this way, concealed; let me always be embarrassed, knowing that you know that I know, but pretend not to know.

---

3 One thing the great poet confessed before biting into her dough-nut: a good poem writes itself as if it doesn't care—never let on that within this finite space, your whole being is heavy with a need to emote infinitely.

4 I never uttered that loose word; I only said, "I opened my legs and let him."

5 One thing the great poet would never confess was that afterwards, she took me into the back room and slapped me for loving her.

6 The picture above represents the moral states of being. The student of art should be particularly cautious of interpreting such depictions without proper background training, as it is often easy to confuse source light with light from another world, as in movies when it is easy to confuse internal sound with external sound.[a] Sometimes, the artist, as does the director, plays tricks for symbolic purposes.[b]

> [a] In cinematic terms, "actual sound" refers to sound which comes from a visible or identifiable source★ within the film. "Commentative sound" is sound which does not come from an identifiable source within the film but is added for dramatic effect.★★
>
> [b] See footnote 1.
>
> > ★ By "identifiable source" it is meant that there exists a presupposition, an understanding that an opposing "unidentifiable source" exists.
> >
> > ★★ By "commentative sound" it is meant that there exists a presupposition, an understanding of a "commentator" who is thereby executing the "commentary."

7 The visit to the circus is of particular import if one considers this passage from a letter written to the man whom she regarded as her guardian angel (to whom she also dedicated a great number of poems). Dated in her 23rd year, the letter states:

> . . . I told Lousine that I was terrified of clowns, no, not just child-ishly afraid like being afraid of the dark, but really, really fearful, like starting-your-period-for-the-first-time scared. Anyhow, she looked at me serious-like and made me promise in that strong Armenian-Brooklyn way of hers that I would never reveal this to anyone because anyone could be an enemy. She made me swear up and down and on graves and holy books and the needle in the eye and all sorts of crazy shit that drove me insane. I can't help but think now that something bad is waiting to happen and that there's this little man staring at me from between the fence slats. I can see his little eyeball sometimes, showing up in the various holes in my apart-ment. But you know what scares me the most? It's that clown in Anthony and Cleopatra who says to Cleopatra, "You must not think I am so simple but I know the devil himself will not eat a woman. I know that a woman is a dish for the gods, if the devil dress her not. But truly, these same whoreson devils do the gods great harm in their women; for in every ten that they make, the devils mar five." So you see, Andy, I have been seriously stressed. Am I marred? Eric says he cannot love me now and that I have a dark side he is afraid of . . .

8 It wasn't that the ice-cream man came everyday; he came whenever the child heard his music.

9 The confessions denoted here are lies, as it would be senseless to list my true regrets. The true regrets are indexed under the subject heading "BUT EVERYONE DIES LIKE THIS," found at the end of the text.

10 Given this information, the definition of "footnote" is of particular interest to the overall understanding of "bedlam." Consider for instance, this denotation: n.2. Something related to but of lesser importance than a larger work or occurrence.

11 See also De Sica's Bicycle Thief; thus the leitmotif of this body: What will I have found in the end if I am seeking as if I am seeking one thing in particular?

12 The great pre-Socratic philosopher Empedocles did not keep the commentative sound of his life a secret. He says of the source of mortal things, one should "know these things distinctly, having heard the story from a god" (As told by Simplicius, Commentary on Aristotle's Physics 160.1–1 = 31B23).

13 It should be understood that Heraclitus also lost a bicycle. In Miscellanies (2.17.4 = 22B18), Clement of Alexandria quotes Heraclitus as saying, "Unless he hopes for the unhoped for, he will not find it, since it is not to be hunted out and is impassable."

14 I Corinthians 13:5 "Doth not behave itself unseemly, seeketh not her own, is not easily provoked, thinketh no evil"; 13:7 "Beareth all things, believeth all things, hopeth all things, endureth all things"; 13:11 "When I was a child, I spake as a child, I understood as a child, I thought as a child: but when I became a woman, I put away childish things"; 13:12 "For now we see through a glass, darkly; but then face to face: now I know in part; but then shall I know even as also I am known." Given these passages, it is easy for the reader to infer that the protagonist, aside from despising her pubic hair, also believed that she was being watched and thus began her odd behavior of hiding and casting her voice into a void.

15 Ms. Boully must have been confused, as it was actually _____, not _____, who uttered "_____" and thus became such a symbolic figure in her youth; however, critic and playwright Lucia Del Vecchio (who is known to transcribe some of her dialogue directly from audiocassettes she and Boully recorded during their undergraduate years) argues that Boully was well acquainted in _____. As this is a suspicious oversight, Del Vecchio cites evidence from a recorded conversation where Boully argues _____.

16 Although the text implies a great flood here, know this is seen through a child's eyes, and here she actually played in sprinklers while loving Heraclitus: "A lifetime [or eternity] is a child playing, playing checkers; the kingdom belongs to a child" (Hippolytus, Refutation 9.9.4 = 22B52).

17 Although the narrative is rich with detail and historical accounts, the author is blatantly supplying false information. For example, the peaches were not rotten and there were no flies or rain for that matter. The man she claims to have kissed never existed, or rather, the man existed; however, she never kissed him, and because she never kissed him, she could only go on living by deluding herself into believing that he never existed.

18 The last time I saw the great poet, I brought her strawberries, hoping she would ask me to bed. Instead, she only suggested that I touch how soft her fuzzy pink sweater was. I broke down crying as soon as I made my confession. I told her that I had written a bad poem, that in the space between me and him, I emoted, through speech and touch, too much and I made it known that I was willing to emote infinitely; the poem was so bad, he left. I was hoping that the great poet would kiss me then, but instead, she slapped me again and forbade me from telling anyone that I was her student. I left her, and I never told her that I was on my hands and knees, picking those berries for her.

19 After the author's death, it was Tristram who went through her various papers and came across the many folders labeled "footnotes." It wasn't until years later, when he was curious as to which papers the footnotes corresponded that Tristram discovered that the "footnotes" were actually daily journals of the author's dreams. Del Vecchio recalls a later audiocassette recording with the author saying, "I have it all worked out. I write down my dreams because I understand them once symbols become written. They're all so sexually charged and I almost always feel ugly in them; they're embarrassing and filthy. But I have it all worked out. No one will know. I've relabeled everything in my study, including my books—you think you're getting Shakespeare, but really, it's astrophysics and cosmology or you open Hesse and you actually get Kierkegaard. I'm not so off am I? But really, I must confess . . ." Del Vecchio, in her words, says, "And then she started going on and on about this Robert Kelly[c] guy."

> [c] The following excerpt from Robert Kelly's "Edmund Wilson on Alfred de Musset: The Dream" was pasted above the author's various beds in the various places she lived: "Dreams themselves are footnotes. But not footnotes to life. Some other transactions they are so busy annotating all night long."

20 Besides the obvious lost marbles or stolen purse or misplaced lottery ticket, the theme of loss preoccupied her even in sleep. The following is from a dream dated in the author's 33rd year:

> (But then, I remembered in my dream that this was only a dream and that when you lose something in a dream, when you wake up, you realize it's still there. Of course, the reverse is true as well, as when I dreamt I had silver eyes and wings, but upon waking up, upon looking into the mirror, I discovered brown eyes, no wings. So, in my dream, I woke up from my dream in my dream, thereby correcting the situation on my own.
>
> This reminds me of Kafka's *Trial*, in a passage deleted by the author: ". . . it is really remarkable that when you wake up in the morning you nearly always find everything in exactly the same place as the evening before.")

21 Ezra Pound: Questing and passive. . . . /"Ah, poor Jenny's case' . . .

from *Seneca Review*

Ballad of
the Comely Woman

◇   ◇   ◇

As I walked out one day
I met on my path a woman
ugly as sin and walking a dog.
She stopped me and said, "Young man,

would you lie with me here
in this field where we're alone,
only my dog as companion?"
The dog went chasing a squirrel.

I placed a hand most gently
on her arm and said, "Old woman,
I've a wife and loving son
dearer to me than my life.

I could not betray such presences."
"Then," she said, "how like you this?"
and stepping to me her limbs grew slim,
her bare breasts brushed my chest.

O love, more than my hair stood on end,
and the grass looked so very green
I could not resist lying down
with her beneath me. "What if,"

I said between our kisses, "you change
again?" "I'm always the same," she said,
and therewith I was left with my face
in the sod and my own restless heart.

from *Beloit Poetry Journal*

What I Threw into the Grave

◇   ◇   ◇

how can I help it
good moonlight, bad rain,
Carl, dusk, picture
of Carl at dusk with
Mona in the background
partially thumbed out,
an unnecessary angel,
the necessary mop,
shadow of the mop,
ten pages covered
in typescript with
the words I'm leaving

this museum/that museum
the cruel sea the mariner's
decoy I stole while housesitting
verbatim, apparition,
a twilight, piece of a meteor
from a childhood summer
in Yarmouth, Nova Scotia,
a pencil to draw the
way to you and the way
back, "we work with
life therefore because
of that work we are

closer to death,"
socks, a fear
of drowning, a love
for staying on the
open road, a boundary
(just on the outside
chance you'll need a
boundary), help, leaves
(a few), 5 red bottles,
a small window,
an evening, good
rain, cruel sea.

from *jubilat*

ANNE CARSON

Opposed Glimpse
of Alice James, Garth James,
Henry James, Robertson James
and William James

◇　◇　◇

("traces of some scene that the newspapers would have characterized as lively")

> *I am glad you like adverbs—I adore them; they are the only qualifications I really much respect and I agree . . . in thinking that the sense for them is the literary sense.*
> *—Henry James, letter to a young admirer, 1902*

A Sunday terrible in all the little ways that Sunday is terrible news.
Home gust of every hour settling sacredly into its custodiary bruise.
Words like buckle-hole and bleat.
The mind's eye.
The mind has no eye.
Aunt Kate sitting alone downstairs.
Without any dinner, as she does not eat.

from *The Threepenny Review*

On the Screened Porch

◇   ◇   ◇

Suppertime. Corn, cooked—some milk
in the water—always threatens to boil over. You let those ears
stand, when it's seethed, two minutes. More tender, that way.
My mother and I

at summer's edge, the garden not as it was, but
lush, intensely green, the lawn's near perfect.
She says, "I love the shadows long"—

    Roof angle, oak trunk, golden chain, extending
    that moment a tree-clinging bird
    creeps along one branch's underside, gleaning the bark—

No need for light overhead, to see
the cloth's rosy pattern,

a familiar mild clicking of cubes: as a child
I was proud to carry in my father's iced coffee and pour,
from the Russel Wright jug, his dollop: the cream,
descending

in meanders, like memory
downward, the liquid's dark bitterness gone.

from *Poetry*

Lullaby for Cuckoo

◇   ◇   ◇

Did you suffer, or was it just the one who made you?
Little bird, deluded or self-deluded,
close your eyes, and let these chirps resound
mechanically. Was vision the clue you lacked,
when emerging from the works you sang sweetly
of midnight, though it was purple noon
and purple riot ran through you, while
the big hand batted and rocked around
the clock, and you alone had time for me?
Or was homo faber the missing link
who forged you in his workshop of stupid toys?
Either way, the little hand is catching up,
the door is opening; you aren't coming out.

from *Skanky Possum*

Corpus Delicti

◊ ◊ ◊

This is the body I will have to die in
having no other while I walk the earth.
Now, as I speak, he is coming from the oblivion
of sleep, dumb almost as he was at birth.
But he ages decades in seconds:
the eyelids lift a crack, commanded by the brain;
the world is rising, light at the window beckons;
whatever I am will be undergone again.
Now my nakedness stands up, the floor is very cold.
Head, heart, hands, cock, legs are growing old
in harmony, this body tells me. We work together.
A time will come we will refuse, we're told
by that authority above us whom we hold
in absolute trust. Death is our master, Peter.

from *Pleiades*

CLARK COOLIDGE

Traced Red Dot

◇   ◇   ◇

Hello I'm Jack Jerk
I live with Molly Ringwald in a hutch
the streets outside the Barleycorn Stretch
they burst it all slims down to a point
a golden gingerale of rockhewn source
buy Grotex it helps your cusp
always thought a corpse would tell me what to do
skin pulling its surface moisture
Barbizon sauce personality like a peanut
just need a new parrot and sink a pressure capsule
grotesque what happens to the lasted soul
a bad mouth liver pills in short bursts
maybe nothing but shirt in strong daylight
a punk trains his fist on the green monkey
it's Bruce Surtees capturing latent death
stacked along contention lines black gleam salt
he's now contented he saw his wrist
rosy featured landschaft grass as a pointer
this all comes from one hand's limited desk
clear before the metal starts flying

from *New American Writing* and *Jacket*

Long after (Mallarmé),

◇ ◇ ◇

irony and pity, some ghosts, some
little pictures of ghosts, some
ancient visual
history of ghosts, livid ghosts and
tiny ghosts, ghosts of rubies
ghosts of diamonds. Once politique,
not any more. You can't say
it that way. Not any more. Ghostly
light of appropriation. Appropriate
ghost. Sad clown, you are
nothing possible. What's a dot com
anyway? Nothing that was. (I say)
I could sit all day, cat
at my feet. Assertion as
comfort, certain as death.
Appropriate garden,
leafy leaf. Can't see
at all. Small
child on the water, can't
see at all.
Fabricated landscape,
can see it all
jar, hill.
Prior encounter,
fall. What will dot com?
Nothing that is.

Cloud, power of ten.
Poem Zero. Hello.

from *3rd Bed*

Midsummer

◇   ◇   ◇

Apex
    of light,
        confusion of greens
Delightful
      shadows of windless
(windlass)   heat
moving over
      the waters.

Prayer of the stillness of noon.
A pause at the balancing point
Grace of the ascent,
        grace of the descent
Hook of fire   proffering
        (chalice) cup
Hair turn
     in shelter
        of the spilling mountains.

Prayer of the grace of noon.
         The sand
vitrifies.
    The glass
      is rainbows.

Whom does the Grail serve?

from *Barrow Street*

THEODORE ENSLIN

Moon Cornering

◊   ◊   ◊

How the corners of the moon
replace themselves.
It is difficult to see
or if I see to say
that this is what I have
seen. Many chances in the lattice
of the winter branches.
Well I've said it and
perhaps there were no corners
after all.

from *Chicago Review*

O Patriarchy

◇　◇　◇

Inaccessible
　　and remote

behind the drawbridge
of the penis.

Who knows
how your contracts
sprang up

without a word,
natural as rain.

The instituation
of you speaks
for all man kindly,

but if a woman
is offended,
she finds no one there
to blame.

from *Skanky Possum*

Animals out of the Snow

◇ ◇ ◇

When snow falls deeply,
mountainously, curvaceously,
animals begin to nudge forth . . .

Caryl and I were visiting the young poet Stephen Smith
in the world of 3 A.M.,
I was generating organs for a new book.
We were invited, as if for a cottage
or mountain cabin stay, but the beds were uneven,
things were tilting, for hours it seemed,
I worried about my throat and
the corpse of John Logan
putting itself into my throat.

At some point it was clear:
Stephen had lost control,
his pets would not behave, would not
let us sleep. Logan, according to Kessler,
was so incapacitated, near the end of his life,
that he lived in an armchair.
Bandit students wandered in and out of his ruined lord,
taking his penis here and there.
Caryl and I were increasingly nargled,
Stephen and Karen had vanished, the animals were
more and more active, angry, would
not let us sleep, slightly fantastic
then beaver-dog bizarre,

cat covered with nipples, a pumice-faced
zippered pug,
                    so I had to get us out,
we were now in a vast urban morgue
(earlier that day
our pantry began to drip,
snow on the roof produced yellow swellings off
    the upper moulding,
splot tears,   Caryl put out pans)

There are dream blasts that annul both
imagination and memory,
I was carrying Caryl nearly naked, blue and stiff,
carrying her like a forward-thrust figurehead
    torn from its bow,
then we were back at Stephen's, with the beasts—
they increased, no one could handle them,
blind hogs, serpentine chows,
tiny striped carnivores, snake-headed chihuahuas—
as Thomas might have said: it was early it was Adam . . .
I was scared out of my dream into
an exploding morgue of animal underdream,
so we fled again,
                    finding ourselves by
a charred plantation by which
blacks were hunched on benches,
    "we can't help you" they said,
oh they were poorer than we, so
again we turned back, into

a stable aflame with molar loads,
with the lords of animal revenge?
I had no rudder, could not make myself awake
and start a new dream or
simply the Zukofsky codex
("we are going to sleep to sleep")
the quarrel, until I stabbed a hyena, was
out of ego's bathysphere,

again I woke, begging to be awake,
Caryl had flung off her comforter,
spread-eagled in nighty,   sleeping soundly.

from *Skanky Possum*

Drones and Chants

◇ ◇ ◇

In memory of Armand Schwerner

All night long they turned the wheels,
picked up the sound and passed it on

All night long we listened to the music,
all night there was thunder among the hills

All night and day the words were spoken,
each word inscribed and traced to its origin

All night and day the words were sung,
picked up, inscribed, and passed along

So as forever to be forgotten,
rising and breaking against the air

The sound floated above the valley
like mist gathering over deep pools

The mist rose above the trees in the valley,
blooming into emblems of silence

Emblems of mist and emblems of trees,
cast forever into the pools of night

The instruments were gathered up from the pools
and all night long they turned the wheels.

from *Hambone*

JEFFREY FRANKLIN

To a Student Who Reads "The Second Coming" as Sexual Autobiography

◇ ◇ ◇

Reading your essay, I find the "widening gyre"
Might be Maud Gonne's; falcon and falconer,
The disaffected lovers who can't hold
The bittersweet anarchy of their world
After her "blood-dimmed tide" is loosed, and everywhere
Illusions of lost innocence are drowned.
Lovers, you say ("the best ones like the worst"!),
Are blinded by passionate intensity.

Surely, to claim a second coming's at hand
Bodes well for romance; on the other hand,
It smacks of locker-room bravado, a lout
Who thinks his "vast image" a *Spiritus Mundi*
Rising again, unsated, for dessert,
His prowess more a lion's than average man's,
His "slow thighs" moving. Yes, that pitiless sun
Might signify his coldness after it,
Her indignation's reeling desert birds
As he rolls over to a stony sleep.
More than leaving her to rock the cradle
Of unprotected sex, that twice he didn't last
For her to finish, you close, "cannot be borne."

from *New England Review*

Independence Day

◇ ◇ ◇

For Paul Beatty

Our huddled masses
Just can't wait
For the pie—

Hole in the
Sky to operate
The soft ice—

Cream cone machine.
Let freedom bling
Bling, Shaq. Like

A dripping Popsicle
Torn in half.
One nation under

God knows what
Thumb, with liberty
Bell souvenirs for

All.

from *Can We Have Our Ball Back?*

Surreal Love Life

◊　◊　◊

Someone who appeared,
head leveled, a disgrace
for public relations. Determined,
a woman as centerpiece
to the domination of owls. Each sweet
sway
encourages designation
as the favored wineshop.
Entropy in clusters
figures in F.'s calculation:
the swim of soup
in the mind's cadaver.

One can go from stutter
to cadence
and call it a theory
of accidentals.
F.'s thought winks
at his fellow
headblazers.
Why did Freud brood except to please
his young lovers, who
slept
in the cellars?
Beyond which there is no
wife
older than she can be.

Yet if F. loved
no one could recognize it
in the sexual attitudes
         of his blue papers.
He troubled the air
         by breathing it
         so dominantly.
                  When the story
                           runs out,
         the white-fingered Lord
assumes a special value,
a stalled hypothesis, as if F.
         dreamt in colors.

         The situation retires
         for the night. Martha's sister
is thought to be the woman who
                           leaked
                  into F.'s mouth.
         One attempt
         is never enough to secure
                  the cherry trees.
F. is not unknown to love,
but is old enough to drive
         a strong suspicion.

The surrealists, of course, veered
         into his headlights
         like frigid antelopes.
                  They oiled the unconscious,
                           crossed
                  themselves with red hearts.
They believed in transcendence
         as the name of words.
                  F. was a man of connections,
         a tiger leaping into
                           sunflowers.

         Success doomed them all.
         The French stood in line:

Breton, Desnos, Eluard.
Breezes cooled the hot
　　pastry shops of
　　　　Vienna.
Stravinsky. Picasso.
　　Nijinsky.
None of them ever died, so suddenly
did the world around them empty.
Freud, in his pajamas, still waits
　　in the vestibule
　　　　to greet
Mother Night with questions
and surprising, incurable answers.

from *Hambone*

Carried Across

◇ ◇ ◇

Through vidrio, a riot of birdsong. Whose face
the stranger? High cheek bones, stout chin,
　　　　　　　　　skin the color of cantaloupe rind.
How continuous, erosions in my grammar. Long
negra-azul hair rivering to the *ahh* of her back. Glackety-
grack, a mortar wagon crosses
　　　　　　　　　tile patio.

Black streets, one fruit stand open late: nova of color. Oh
nectarial moon, only elsewhere are you called
cliché. Lovers entwined
　　　　　　　　　on benches.
Low whisper of light
night traffic at the park's edge. What if
　　　　　　　　　"we" did not
　　　　　　　　　　　　presuppose
national, ethnic, linguistic affiliation? What word, then, throw
at the yapping dog?

        Blotting out vision, breathable air, a carbonized foulness
    mushrooms
behind the bus. Her dress fades
       into distance as color
           blown
        onto a resin sequence. Now
are grackles hooked
by the sol's aigrette, disturbed
    and stern and enormous.
        The unstressed fourth and invented fifth foot
   of their long-voweled croaking
       inflames me. By the throatful.
But in this human language, *the world*
is full of voices, I experience
     extended moments of cloud. Will does not limit
what I feel. The pornography is inexhaustible.

Ruina

Casa
Para
Aves

Nido
Para
Amor

Todo
Para
Nada

The cast of her torso—
corset de yeso—sits upright on the bed like a kettle, a seam
cleaving its left side, the molded expression of breasts. Each
pájaro deviates slightly from habitual song
and I listen as though
to answer all.

Vocables unloose
from their reference. Through
unyielding columns of cars,
a deaf mute, red rag in hand, looms—
exhausted face at the windshield.

Or an ebony Christ in San Romano, head
cocked to the wall of retablos, brilliant
appeals left alone
too long. Encontrandose
Eulalia Prado en condicione de perder la vista
imploro a la virgen
de Rorio de Talpa
el cual da gracias por el Beneficio recibido. A lamb
on a huge book, an eagle facing upward, an eye
in a pyramid, and before each symbol on the altar box,
a coin slot. The translation.

Invented their own
writing and vigesimal scale. I am, *crumbled
dust.* In 69 A.D.,
the glyphic script indicates, Ah Cracaw
took Jaguar Paw
prisoner. Plopped his children in clay vessels, a jade bead
in each mouth. Across cleavage planes
in his earrings, my reflection splays,
my obsidian-
pupiled eyes.

Fifteen ways of perforating and filing the teeth,
encrusted
with gems
carved from limestone, basalt,
pyroclastic rock. All but three
Mayan codices
were burned
to clear the slab for Christ. Truth
is structured, I scribbled, like language.
Which language? Hill of grasshoppers. Altar
of skulls. Said of her own work that sincerity
and veracity are distinct. Has no interest
in sincerity. Ocean of cloud
lapping the volcano.

The unglazed figure reaching behind
to wipe himself. A past that never stops
            changing its meanings. I am alive,
he wrote, and cannot bear
                to be unworthy of my life. Came to the end
        of words and waited. Then *things* restore silence, speaking
only of themselves. Lizards
            lick shadows under the dry fountain. Lidless gaze.
The butt and very dustmark of my utmost journey.
                            Pain as language
        withheld.

On the white stucco wall, a cat
                closes its eyes
        to the clang of machetes in musical phrases
with cigarette pauses
                    for breath. The surround is whistling,
an aggregate sound
with sweet singularities in the flamboyanes. A policeman
smoking against the gate
        of a residencia, Rottweiler
                            heaped by his boots.
        Jacaranda, fuchsia, camellia
pink. Ornithologists know the songs of birds, who
                knows their thoughts? Translation alone
births the untranslatable. Listen, Señor,
                        I have been used
by my own ignorance, my self-disgust, my instinct
for failure. Pray for me.

Every poem suggests it, suggests its own—
                    Coffined in, the bus weaving
dim streets. And then dawn begins
to colonize the space
around me, to colorize distance: trees greening, light
          parceling out sinople walls and roofs
                              going ocher before
                                        the spectral,
dusty highway. Words ripen my difference
from the world. Spasms
          burrowing into my eye.

Incomparable odor from the tortilleria, yeasty-flour
sour blue-baked smoke flavors the air. Two teenage girls
bunch beneath the yellow and white umbrella.
                              Workman
in a hole in the road, a parasol
on its side shading him. Forepaw bandaged,
a dog observes from the esquino,
near the emptied jail.
                    What language
does not incarnate presence? Just a moment,
Señor, executioner.
                    The barber

sleeps in a cane chair outside his shop. Musics mixing
        paratactically along cobbled streets. In high heels,
women tracked by furtive eyes
        from the portales. Torqued grotesquely
                        and biting its own rump in the park. A form
                                        of meditation for me.
Like pheromone trails traced by ants, the meeting places
of glances. And every moment around the zócalo,
        expectancy of more arrivance. Picking a fresh scab
            above the hairline of my neck.
Only some red

            and blue wash and the figures of a family drawing
        their own blood. Two thousand years gone, a hand
paused before this naked lintel, thinking. A hand
                            in my mind.
                    The sign
announces Basura Peatonal "walking rubbish." Of things ill done
        and done to others' harm. Marta, Paula, Lope,
and Alima Alma raced to the top of the temple pyramid, HERE
                        to graffiti their names.
Swallows rake the field,
mesmerizing me. To read the script
of their flight is to conceive in parabolas. Rhythms combing out
knots of habit. Face to the wall,
the haircut costs sixty pesos. Who would not pay eighty
                for a haircut with landscape?

        from *Kenyon Review*

Beginning with a Phrase from Simone Weil

◇   ◇   ◇

There is no better time than the present when we have lost everything. It doesn't mean rain falling
at a certain declension, at a variable speed is without purpose or design.
The present everything is lost in time, according to laws of physics things shift
when we lose sight of a present,
when there is no more everything. No more presence in everything loved.

In the expanding model things slowly drift and everything better than the present is lost in no time.
A day mulches according to gravity
and the sow bug marches. Gone, the hinge cracks, the gate swings a breeze,
breeze contingent upon a grace opening to air,
velocity tied to winging clay. Every anything in its peculiar station.

The sun brightens as it bleaches, fades the spectral value in everything seen. And chaos is no better model
when we come adrift.
When we have lost a presence when there is no more everything. No more presence in everything loved,
losing anything to the present. I heard a fly buzz. I heard revealed nature,

cars in the street and the garbage, footprints of a world, every fly
a perpetual window,
    unalloyed life, *gling,* pinnacles of tar.

    There is no better everything than loss when we have time. No
lack in the present better than everything.
    In this expanding model rain falls
    according to laws of physics, things drift. And everything better
than the present is gone
    in no time. A certain declension, a variable speed.
    Is there no better presence than loss?
    A grace opening to air.
    No better time than the present.

from *Boston Review*

Reunion

◇   ◇   ◇

It is discovered, after twenty years, they like each other,
despite enormous differences (one a psychiatrist, one a city official),
differences that could have been, that were, predicted:
differences in tastes, in inclinations, and, now, in wealth
(the one literary, the one entirely practical and yet
deliciously wry; the two wives cordial and mutually curious).
And this discovery is, also, discovery of the self, of new capacities:
they are, in this conversation, like the great sages,
the philosophers they used to read (never together), men
of worldly accomplishment and wisdom, speaking
with all the charm and ebullience and eager openness for which
youth is so unjustly famous. And to these have been added
a broad tolerance and generosity, a movement away from any contempt or
     wariness.
It is a pleasure, now, to speak of the ways in which
their lives have developed, alike in some ways, in others
profoundly different (though each with its core of sorrow, either
implied or disclosed): to speak of the difference now,
to speak of everything that had been, once, part
of a kind of hovering terror, is to lay claim to a subject. Insofar
as theme elevates and shapes a dialogue, this one calls up in them (in its
     grandeur)
kindness and good will of a sort neither had seemed, before,
to possess. Time has been good to them, and now
they can discuss it together from within, so to speak,
which, before, they could not.

from *Slate*

The Gold Star

◊　◊　◊

Elaine's job on the geriatric ward included encouraging
the constipated to loose their stingy, gnarled marbles
into the bowl—by hand: there wasn't anything more tenderly
conducive than an orderly's gloved fingers.
There's nothing redeeming in this. Simply: she
needed the pay, they needed her excavating
(literally: *from out / of their cavities*) help.
The rest?—"an alien stink that followed me home,
under my toenails, in my hair." But surely we'd do it
willingly for someone that we loved . . . yes? Even
gratefully—for someone that we loved. And then
we'd clean the pad, we'd rinse it free of its gobbets
the size and color of cornelian cherries . . .
gladly, yes? Gladly and changed. Better;
tested. Even when my mother was dying,
shrinking, growing hard rosettes
as if her lungs were tanks in an experiment . . .
didn't I tend to her? and wasn't it the way
it always used to be?—that with precision instinct
she'd arranged this just so she could prove
to relatives and neighbors that her son
was so caring, her son was the best. I'd wring
the compress, set it on her forehead again.
What a good boy I was!

from *The Antioch Review*

DONALD HALL

Affirmation

◇　◇　◇

To grow old is to lose everything.
Aging, everybody knows it.
Even when we are young,
we glimpse it sometimes, and nod our heads
when a grandfather dies.
Then we row for years on the midsummer
pond, ignorant and content. But a marriage,
that began without harm, scatters
into debris on the shore,
and a friend from school drops
cold on a rocky strand.
If a new love carries us
past middle age, our wife will die
at her strongest and most beautiful.
New women come and go. All go.
The pretty lover who announces
that she is temporary
is temporary. The bold woman,
middle-aged against our old age,
sinks under an anxiety she cannot withstand.
Another friend of decades estranges himself
in words that pollute thirty years.
Let us stifle under mud at the pond's edge
and affirm that it is fitting
and sweet to lose everything.

from *The New Yorker*

MICHAEL S. HARPER

TCAT serenade: 4 4 98 (New Haven)

◇   ◇   ◇

30th anniversary of MLK, Jr.'s killing;
the cure to come

the wound of race as metaphor
in Seamus Heaney's TCAT

what he calls Homer's Ghost
and where the black heart of hope

reside in future
in the arc of history

as dramaturg, as bard, as sage
as only in a lover's hold

where rape incest
miscegenation

can be embraced as play
as useless curiosity

the anthropologists
store up as details

for the compass
of compassion

as prism
understanding

action
morality

grace
under extreme pressure

art
life

4 Little Girls
notes from a Birmingham jail

can be the cure at Troy
Philoctetes

with bow that never misses its mark
will break the arc

and let the other
speak

from *Harvard Review*

you: should be shoo be

◊   ◊   ◊

you could no longer just be
an on
going off
beat drop
out poet in a society
that beat up on you but
never in
cluded you be
doo be
doo be
doo besides
in *blues people* you

had jumped off
your cantilevered cool
score for crane's strusse *bridge*
over deep river's troubled water

larry walked the talk
with you
thru *black fire*
askia toured you
thru ancient ideograms in father
africa's unrolled papyrus scroll
primer: akan & bambara 1-2-3
  -conga (*black music*)
  dogon ewe fanti 1-2-3
  -mojo (*black magic*) you

picked up down
picking banjoed back to kora
it became you to be
a griot you reigned
as chief american nommo mau mau
imamu you sprung us from the 12
bar blues with good news
about our blackness:

aesthetics ethics should be are
one sister brother a ga "ka ba"
(no mo' doo doo)
adinkra dink a doo

spirit house ensouled us
with renewed black heart
minded home tongue
you gave
us all of you we
gave back our ears eyes
collective word

you could no longer be
just another beat
in the music

you booked from
an angry idyll
angst too
hip for words
& broke bad
you blued red
& white to
green black bloods
you remade your

self african as your own on
call for us to pick up hand carved fist
topped ebony lickin' sticks to drum
a steeled peace for our self

warring selves just up from
wholly stolen cargo people
shipped across holy water
by the dirty dozens
to many thousand hellish places
via the good ship *zong* the *phillis* the *power*
& the *glory*
east to west

left of wright
the body of your work read red (will
never be a corpse &) always
plays "the bridge" be

tween yesterday & tomorrow:

to truly live you must
be your poetry
which should be is
your politics
your aesthetics
your ethic
your ethos world

view too you
can't just
chant justice you struggle
don't just
say write unity you

need to must
be & do be
more than an imitation of
your imitators' shoo be doo be doo's

& by the dozens hundreds
thousands tens of thousands
we by rite rewrote
our reality renamed ourselves named
our children kamal nneke kalonji

nia kimba ayan reza
thought lived worked word
play clay africanized
the national hive's domesticated doo
be drone bees we became us
on our own heady raw black honey &
x'd old double crosses burned into our brains with cross

pollinated poems
potent stinger pens
to protect ourselves by more
than any dreams necessary

to span the gulf home you
spun ananse's black silk cocoon to keep us
from the tacky white tar
baby's fly paper *declaration*
yankee doodle lie

you webbed the hood with barricades
of barbed wire words
sharp as the *amistad*'s cane knives "sos"
suspension cables of consciousness
from burning cities' melted country
blues steel guitars that had played
the bridge so many thousand

crossed over so baraka
so long ago
& all along you
so becomingly voice(d) our various
righteous right on power
to the people 60's 70's selves

out of your personal middle

passages you put down the pan pipe
cleared your hudson river reed of self
pith
freely tenored an old call
in another register

another key as we pitched
boxes full of forked tongue tea
leaves off the george washington bridge

you long since wrote all that was
word possible made worldwide earthtoned
connections your discordant choral chords
rearrange received histories'
choke hold languages' sour noted suite
of rum sung barracoon sea chanteys

here's to you for
having borne and delivered so many
of us as
eulogies before our after
elegies praise songs
for yet another invoked dead *bad* blood
spirit for uninvited

(an' aint i a poet)

black warrior women 60's poets
in their 60's & 70's
you walked out on "on"'s
last free verse line left

. . . to live your poetry
with your african/native
american/poet/life
partner you went to the nearby reservation where
you saw read thought about:
  academic bounty scalps
  multicolored indian corn
  nat turner's tanned skin red
  rice recently cut off
  cured blackened rind yellow
  souvenir ears of the empire's
  more recent enemies
  ken saro-wiwa's gavel beaten black
  & blue tongue put in a mason

dixon jar of crude palm wine refined
tourists sip from old black gold
coast scallop shells one american
oklahoma bomb decades after
bombed burned down black tulsa killed
more people than all
those long burning 60's city summers
but not as many
as the 1898 ghost dance
or 1943 camp van dorn
mississippi massacres for national security

TERRORISM IS AS AMERICAN
AS BLACK TESTICLE PIE

the totem of broken word stolen
land penn's indian treaty
lynching tree the pulsing promise
in the masses of unbroken people yesterday

today & tomorrow . . . as always

at each reading you
return to us renewed
stand up before us
blow red white black
and blue facts as gainsay
into the masked face of lone ranger racism
loudly read your "amerika" state

of the black art scat
"cherokee" from here
to "come sunday" hum *home* by way
of our elevated underground railroad
. . . *systems* . . . thru trane's "alabama" modulate "afrika"
to a brassy bravura based
on the internationale
without one corny shoo be doo be doo

from *Crux*

9-11-01

◇ ◇ ◇

The first person is an existentialist

Like trash in the groin of the sand dunes
Like a brown cardboard home beside a dam

Like seeing like things the same
Between Death Valley and the desert of Pavan

An earthquake a turret with arms and legs
The second person is the beloved

Like winners taking the hit
Like looking down on Utah as if

It was Saudi Arabia or Pakistan
Like war-planes out of Miramar

Like a split cult a jolt of coke New York
Like Mexico in its deep beige couplets

Like this, like that . . . like call us all It,
Thou It. "Sky to Spirit! Call us all It!"

The third person is a materialist.

from *Can We Have Our Ball Back?*

RONALD JOHNSON

◊ ◊ ◊

across dark stream
of shooting stars

supplicant cast fly
another year alive

belief, belief brief
zero at white core

from *Hambone*

Flying

◇ ◇ ◇

When Mother was little, all
that she knew about flying was what
her bearded grandfather told her:
every night your soul flies
out of your body and into
God's lap. He keeps it under
his handkerchief until morning.

Hearing this as a child haunted me.
I couldn't help sleeping.
I woke up each morning groping
as for a lost object lodged perhaps
between my legs, never knowing
what had been taken from me or what
had been returned to its harbor.

When as a new grandmother
my mother first flew cross-country—
the name of the airline escapes me
but the year was 1947—
she consigned her soul to the Coco-
Chanel-costumed stewardess
then ordered a straight-up martini.

As they landed, the nose wheel wobbled
and dropped away. Some people screamed.
My mother was not one of them
but her shoes—she had slipped them off—
somersaulted forward. Deplaning

she took out her handkerchief
and reclaimed her soul from the ashen stewardess.

That night in a room not her own
under eaves heavy with rain
and the rue of a disbelieving daughter
my mother described her grandfather to me:
a passionate man who carried his soul
wedged deep in his pants' watch-pocket
a pious man whose red beard had never seen scissors,

who planted his carrots and beets
in the dark of the moon for good reason
and who, before I was born,
rose up like Elijah.
Flew straightaway up into heaven.

from *Connecticut Review*

Great

◇　◇　◇

We cross into the great & there goes
you know. There's a voice stream, she
& I can fly up, holding on to air. I
blue, queer as folk, get the best home
cooking there. Sent me this great card
sd Art is Forever, & I wrote back Whatever.
Here, do I slink around, my fellow felons.
There, & my cockles & mussels, & I hunger
for love, or what passes for, according to
Dotty, Dots, Dorothy for short. Impossible
words become worlds, as we round a mountain
where the blue air's hung. There's nothing
no, about your arms, not yet, don't think. In-
stead, I hum, as if about to burst into the tiniest
of song, & sometimes I wing it, unsure, unsung
& anonymous, & comes out mumbles, like
marbles, whose halls I roam. These great
great cities, as they pass away before me, all
shiny & swoony. Somewhere, sometimes I'll
think before I squeak, & somewhere sometimes
why I simply leap, as toward you, I just leap.

from *Boondoggle*

"Broken World"
(For James Assatly)

◇　◇　◇

1

faith and rain
　　　brightness falls

　　　blank as glass
　　　　　brightness falls

　　　until he

can't bend
　　　light anymore.

　　　Won't be stronger. Won't be water.
Won't be dancing or floating berries.
Won't be a year. Won't be a song.
Won't be taller. Won't be accounted
a flame. Won't be a boy. Won't be
any relation to the famous rebel.

You are with me
　　　and I shatter

everyone who
　　　hates you.

Arrows on water;
　　　you are with me—

rain on snow—
    and I shatter

everyone who
    hates you.

2

To be a man, to be, to try. I hate the word *man*. I'm not crazy about the word *husband* or the word *father* either. To try. To heal the night or day. I'm busy selling fighters and bombers. The NASDAQ moves in my face. I'm wired to my greasy self-portrait. Every day in every way. America equals ghost. The wrong side of history. Flat matted yellow weeds. Who could believe "God chose me." Flat matted yellow weeds. God chose? You were dying that spring. Reading at some college I saw ROTC boys in fatigues. The talkiness of winter unwraps me now. In each room someone is fingering her or his soul. The talkiness of winter unwraps me now. The garden made unknowing by the snow. Erased by snow. Erased by snow. Two blocks from campus, a boy, maybe ten or eleven, yelled at a Junior High School girl: "Ho-bag, incest baby, spread your legs." It's all naked out here. Nothing is here. It's all one big strip mall. We have a Ponderosa.

3

faith and rain
    brightness falls

    blank as glass
        brightness falls

Won't be the magic
lantern or dancer.
Won't be despite
the fullness of time,
the other three magic ones.
Won't be a year. Won't be a song.
Won't be a beginning.
Won't be forward.
Won't be on the way.
Won't be a dreary prison.

Won't be the month of May.
Won't be Mary. Won't be the sea road.
Won't be stronger.
Won't be younger.
Won't be pink. Won't be opening from under.

The word.
        The word of God.

The word of God
        in a plastic bag.

I couldn't hear.
        I couldn't hear

your voice.
        You are with me

and I shatter
        everyone who

hates you.
        Arrows on water;

you are with me—
        rain on snow—

and I shatter
        everyone who

hates you.
        faith and rain

brightness falls
        blank as glass

        brightness falls

from *Colorado Review*

Felix Culpa

◇   ◇   ◇

Down on all fours.

The breaking of rules
the only rule.

Cut off from clear lines
of retreat.

Beguiled by excess.

By like-minded folk
enthroned

in ever tinier courts.

from *Ploughshares*

On Antiphon Island

◇   ◇   ◇

—"mu" twenty-eight part—

On Antiphon Island they lowered
the bar and we bent back. It
wasn't limbo we were in albeit
  we limbo'd. Everywhere we
                        went we
  limbo'd, legs bent, shoulder
   blades grazing the dirt,
                   donned
andoumboulouous birth-shirts,
  sweat salting the silence
we broke . . . Limbo'd so low we
  fell and lay looking up at
  the clouds, backs embraced by
                     the
ground and the ground a fallen
                 wall
  we were ambushed by . . . Later we'd
  sit, sipping fig liqueur, beckoning
sleep, soon-come somnolence nowhere
  come as yet. Where we were, not-
withstanding, wasn't there . . .

                Where we
were was the hold of a ship we were
                  caught
in. Soaked wood kept us afloat . . . It
wasn't limbo we were in albeit we

limbo'd our way there. Where we
were was what we meant by "mu."

                    Where
we were was real, reminiscent
arrest we resisted, bodies briefly
                        had,
held on
to

★

"A Likkle Sonance" it said on the
record. A trickle of blood hung
  overhead I heard in spurts. An
introvert trumpet run, trickle of
                    sound . . .
A trickle of water lit by the sun
  I saw with an injured eye, captive
music ran our legs and we danced . . .
                Knees
bent, asses all but on the floor, love's
  bittersweet largesse . . . I wanted
trickle turned into flow, flood,
  two made one by music, bodied
             edge
gone up into air, aura, atmosphere
  the garment we wore. We were on
a ship's deck dancing, drawn in a
             dream
above hold . . . The world was ever after,
                    elsewhere.
Where we were they said likkle for little, lick
  ran with trickle, weird what we took it
for . . . The world was ever after, elsewhere,
               no
way where we were
was there

from jubilat

And Even You Elephants?

(Stein 139/Titles 35)

◊   ◊   ◊

And even a place?
A sounder one.

Whose hanging showed a desperate resignation?
Recognition and restitution prepare extreme pleasure.
Amusing concentrated heaviness can be splendid.

Circulating cigarettes distinguish resignation.
Exuding recognition won't enlarge all circumstances.
Consider an entirely reasonable description.
Would such a description coagulate recognition?
And what would it express?

Glass.
Four sincerely intentional gliders resigned.
Instruct us to recognize persecution.
Can't all eyes recognize it?
All could.
Nothing's enclosing space, necessity's originary institution.
Which choking explanation is even a sauce for the crestfallen?

We seconded singular eucalyptus preparations.
What preparations?
Isn't that strangely prepared asparagus soup too glassy?
Merciful heating is necessary for cooking.
Have straight descriptions of preparation disappeared?
Can glass establish erections?

[Strophe continued from page 80]

Frequently astonishing cooking restores resignation to birthdays.
Resignation and brushing can be especially wetting conundrums.
Lengthening daylight and preparing for penetration are examples of alleviation.
Would counting plates and burning placards distract a mercenary opportunist?
Can Justice's splendid declarations withstand even you elephants?

from *Deluxe Rubber Chicken*

Source: Gertrude Stein's *Tender Buttons,* first edition, as corrected by Stein in her hand-written entries in Donald Sutherland's copy, found by Ulla E. Dydo in the University of Colorado Library, Boulder. *Seed:* Stein's title "An Elucidation." *Method:* Sending source and seed through DIASTEX5, Charles O. Hartman's 1994 update of his 1989 digital automation of one of my "diastic text-selection" methods (developed in 1963) and revising the output into sentences by changes of word order, affixes, and "helping words." *Form:* Five strophes comprising numbers of verse-line sentences corresponding to the prime-number sequence 2, 3, 5, 7, 11. New York: 28 September–7 November 2000, 22 December 2001.

Perfect Front Door

◊　◊　◊

My summer
is threadbare
these jeans
are chains

always
the sense
of the futility
of maintenance

yet I feel
the cool
night air
from the open door

capital
crosses the border
at will
why not labor.

from *The Hat*

Address to Winnie in Paris

◇ ◇ ◇

Winnie, I am writing this on behalf of my friend Harris. He loves you and wants you to love him. I have never been to Paris, but I have heard that it is a good place to be in love in.

The Arc de Triomphe is real. The Jardin des Tuileries is real. The Eiffel Tower is very real. The carafe of wine, the remains of dinner, the bill: all real. None is necessary to your life.

Harris has confided that he enjoys dating. To profess such a thing is to advertise a facility for one kind of loneliness, which has nothing to do with the other kind: the one you did not know was there until afterward.

The part of the betrayal which wounds the most is hearing that it has already happened.

Diderot wrote that the word is not the thing, but a flash in whose light we perceive the thing. Plato wrote of the need to be reconjoined with the rest of oneself. My analyst speaks of codependent impulses in modern society. These various explanations are metaphors for an inaccessible truth.

In de Laclos, a betrayal is an invitation to a string of further betrayals, each one taking you further from the original. If the hell for lovers consists in being betrayed, the hell for the beloved consists in betraying. These hells constitute the world.

A much older friend writes: Most romances do not last, and it is best to forget them. Tolstoy writes: All happy families are alike. My teacher says: Bad poems are all bad for the same reason: imprecision.

Around you move many seas. It is impossible not to drown a little. In Bulfinch's, an anchor is let down into the garden. This is to remind us that we live underwater.

Up above the high-water mark, angels with their teeth and their sharp little wings watch us with murderous disinterest. They sentence us for the one crime we all commit.

It is said by area doctors that cowboys notoriously misrepresent their degree of pain. For this reason their diseases progress far beyond the point at which treatment is beneficial. Are they lying?

If I could read only one sentence for the rest of my life, it would be the one where the jailer says to Socrates *I can see that you are a good man, the best one that has ever been in this place.*

These examples are meant to dissuade you, Winnie, from loving men other than my friend Harris. He asked me to write this poem.

Arvol Looking Horse, a Sioux leader, called Devils Tower *the heart of everything that is.* Very large objects remind us of the possibility of the infinite, which has no size at all. But we understand it as something very, very large.

What the lover seeks is the possibility of return, the strange heart beating under every stone.

from *jubilat*

Butter & Eggs

◊   ◊   ◊

1

The circular cast-iron skillet, used for nothing else, is an eighth of an inch
    thick
and broad enough to let its contents spread unhindered.

The skillet is set over high heat, its cooking surface greased
with a mild oil, or butter cut with oil, or best of all clarified butter, itself
    pure oil.

Broken into a bowl and salted, two eggs are sprinkled with coarsely chopped
    parsley and chives,
then beaten roundly with a small fork until they twirl in a ring.

The oiled skillet smokes faintly. The beaten eggs, tipped into its center,
sizzle in a circle that tilting widens as desired.
Joggling the skillet shifts the thickening eggs back and forth and at last
slides them to the rim opposite its handle, where the emerging lip
is flipped with the tip of the fork towards the center of the
    circle
and rolled back towards its nearer edge. The opposite edges
may not quite fold shut, but any gap is closed
by neatly overturning the contents of the skillet onto a plate.

On the plate the eggs continue to cook,
so a moist interior in the skillet yields a dry interior on the
    plate
while a moist interior on the plate wants a runny interior in the skillet,

and for a runny interior on the plate the interior in the skillet must be
     disconcertingly soggy.
These facts are variously modified if, across the circle of newly
     poured eggs
(in these cases lacking the speckling of herbs),
mushrooms are aligned, or diced fried lard, or grated tart cheese.

2

Hot water is poured two inches deep into a small pot
that is set covered over a high flame until it boils. The flame is lowered;
a fresh egg, its shell pricked at the rounder end with a medium-fine pin,
is lowered with a spoon into the simmering water; the lid is set back in
     place.
After four minutes the egg is—at sea level—spooned out and rinsed in cold
     water;
at higher altitudes, allowance is made for the progressively lower
     temperatures
at which water boils: ten seconds is added for every thousand feet.
In Santa Fe an egg is not cooked in less than five minutes.

The egg may be broken into a bowl, then buttered and salted;
or set in an egg cup, small end up, in which case the shell
is circularly crackled by tapping with the back of a knife
half an inch below the tip, then opened with a thrust of the blade.
Salting should be restrained but never omitted, as the French maxim implies:
"A kiss without a moustache is like an egg without salt."
A spoon of wood or plastic leaves the savor intact.

3

In a tall three-quart pot, two quarts of water are brought to a boil.
A tablespoon of vinegar is added. The water is stirred with the spoon
in a strong circular stroke that spins it against the sides of the pot
so as to form at its center a vortex whose momentum sustains itself
while an egg is broken into the whirling hollow. Instantly cooked,
the white of the egg enwraps the yolk, restoring a shape
like that of the unbroken shell. Use then determines the time

when the egg must be extracted with a slotted spoon:
whether, dried in paper toweling, it is to be set on a trimmed slice of toast
to be eaten salted, soft, and hot; or, cooled and firm, reserved for immersion
in a ramekin of aspic lined with a thin slice of ham, with two leaves
of blanched tarragon laid crosswise on the congealing stock.

4

A tablespoon of fat—butter, bacon grease, mild oil—is gently warmed
in a small, trustworthy skillet. A lid that can seal the skillet
is placed directly on another flame, set high. Two eggs are broken
into the warmed skillet, with care not to rupture the yolks,
and moderately seasoned with salt and pepper. When the lid
is too hot to touch, it is set over the eggs
and from time to time briefly removed to observe them:
patience and attentiveness are both required
to seize the moment of perfection
when the whites are no longer glairy,
the yolks not yet whitening,
and the eggs are tilted (unstuck if needs be with a rubber spatula)
at once out of the skillet onto the breakfast plate.

5

A tablespoon of oil, bacon grease, or clarified butter
is heated in a medium or large skillet set on the highest possible flame.
Broken into a bowl, two eggs seasoned with salt and pepper
are briefly but strenuously beaten. When the fat sizzles and smokes
at maximum heat, the skillet is withdrawn from the flame,
the eggs are poured into its center and there with a fork or wooden spatula
immediately stirred and turned so that no part of them
stays long in contact with the scorching surface but the whole
is uninterruptedly mixed and remixed until, attaining a soft solidity,
it can be folded upon itself and promptly flipped onto a plate.
Scarcely ten seconds pass between the moment the eggs
touch the skillet and their removal. The flame should be extinguished.

Eight quarter-pound sticks of sweet butter are pressed
into a two-quart double boiler or bain-marie
that is brought to a boil and kept simmering
while the butter softens slowly into a muddled yellowish soup
that gradually separates on three levels: floating at the top,
a layer of foamy casein; a residuum of casein settling
on the bottom; and between them a depth
of clear oil of butter. When these strata are stable,
the flame is extinguished and the upper pot
removed slowly and surely to a counter where it rests
until the casein layers have steadied. The froth
is then skimmed off with a spoon or tea strainer,
and with surpassing gentleness the butter oil is poured
into a jar. The operation may need to be performed
more than once to keep the underlying casein
from slithering over the rim of the pot while one salvages
every possible drop of oil, which afterwards—except
for what is of immediate use—is sealed in its container
and refrigerated. This perfect cooking butter
will not turn rancid and, heated to high temperatures,
never brown or burn: it is the word "blessing" clarified.

from *Boston Review*

DUNCAN MCNAUGHTON

The quarry (1–13)

◇ ◇ ◇

frontispiece

what more than affections can senses tell
in this illness of time   of quantity

words can hardly follow   quickly enough
thought can't wait   to work it orderly out

how much of silence can comedy bear
what ratchet mood knits tighter to its pole

what hour is this   what outer precession
knots a man's heart   so it's dammed against care

our least fortunate   schedule of motions
seemingly plays out

                                   the instant's tipped

meaning wears many names   yours for example
        labyrinth another

    I lose my way

   firing the five senses
       at the leftovers
     strewn behind it
          by the disorientedly
      meandering word

     "and"

                dans l'intérieur de la carrière
        where the stars of night
                                have seemed to make pictures
            là-haut   sur le ciel

                                the passageway
        has narrowed
                            to a regular series of intervals
            or durations
                    blocks of cleanly dressed stone
                                    as far as one can see
                    occlude the dark tunnel
            to divide each progress from the next
                or where we have come from

        at the end of this routinely impeded measure
            of time over each block of which we have to climb
                    framed in a vertical rectangle of
                                    blindingly white light
                    the word "and" hangs
                                        90 degrees off its plane
                    in its furnace   of Cretan sunlight

that the end can be   or may be
                posterior
                    to the impossible

        history told
                        that's bought & sold

            old manse   moss green
                away on the outward shell
                        del árbol permanente

            árbol temblante

                    ᶜAli's tree
                        away on the outward scale
            dipende "and"

    only by its concealment can its form be
                                made to appear

        where hid
                in what tellarium

voluble matter   mother's dream
         every broken-down refrain   breaking down
                  who's to say
              who's more perplexed   or   least incarnate

         features of his father   there in the mirror
     plainest creature yet
                  walks on two feet
         all as I am but the head
                  appended
                  from another leukos brute

still   he feels the setting sun
                  burning ear   I mean
                       the plough
         turning up the dark
                       à la belle étoile

gypsum halls   wherein he wanders
         always wondering
              "and" to "and"

ô transposed head   cobbled or knit
           in whose possession   whose grip
                    our days
             whom else do we ask

       this paradox   of good news
         that its smallness   not   be undetected
                      this paradise at "and"

     in between
                   we swallow the abyss

world   it says   old old man
              adagio
                       easy
experience   what else
      something to remember
                  "and"   the end
                    is less than

         ahora lento

minotaur   leaning on its cane

        poet inside
          the long gallery   mind is

                is he alone
he stops to kneel

       ô gracious friend
    you who loves me
     you whom I love

   after this life
        shall we never be again
           together

   what company   can thus be

tous les jours   six gnossiènes
faisaient une promenade
à la plage

                crest to trough
trough to crest
           cretics laved
              pebbled strand

one of those girls became my mother

they were gathered there   ce joli corps
        des jeunesses
to watch the imposter
        through whom "and" expressed
whose immodest beauty   whose whiteness
        bathe
        in the encircling Deep

before its entrance   its mouth
                         on the beach   one's back to the sea
        a map   drawn in sand

                    but not all of it
                 half has been erased

        by some carelessness   perhaps one's own
        has one stepped where one was uninvited
            had one ever known not to

still   one's expected to know the absent moiety   by heart

question   less of itself   than of whom to ask it

compromised   by one's tactless love
                    by one's bemusement   of dissolutions
            one's ineptitude of schedules   of stations
        by one's clumsy macedonian impatience

                    as if one might pry open the syllable
                              "and"
                as if one could force open the redness
                    of an unwilling rose
            as if its petals might yield their fragrance to mind

        they won't

nor can one return to the boat
                    that brought one to this insulation
                        it's gone

fi'l-Andalūs   the word fegdhoim   signifies
  a breed of dog with the face of a bull's-eye
    a type of winter sweater   knit from wool by a seaman
              a niche   in the city wall
                        where a prostitute sleeps
      ontological illegibility

          a desuetude of white
            contempt
            a witness
        the subjective dilation of an hour
                  an island in the middle of white rain
      the gate of a city wall   beyond which   beach   receives sea
                what love has to do with it
            the bony smile of a smooth white skull
    a woman   sodomized   while drinking beer through a reed
                a wedge
                        the number five
              the Malabar coast
                        a mosaic floor under a high white dome
                            a kiss

  the g is soft   the d silent   the h unaspirated
              of which "and"   divides
                                  into the signs
              for the halves
                      of breathing

           raggedy "and"   borderline
yet the poem's indifference
                              to the disappearance of time
              is everywhere
                   the poet's supernatural love
                            finds its sound

        what the word has cradled   between its horns
                              let the crescent vessel

         there must be a person
                        to have found the way in

          immense stone blocks cut   from stone
                            dressed by labrys

   where are those men if not now upon the sea floor

                the great necropolis
                     aswarm with archaic Greeks
                                    called Mycenaean
          the needle inscribing its fluctuations like that
               on a seismic device or an EKG
                               flattens to a static line
           that contraption Daedalus made for Pasiphaë
                    soon rotted beneath the meadow oak
           that overhangs it in this faded photograph
               she only used its stirrups once

           Knossos overtaken   aswarm with heroes

  in the hour of Hekuba's tears   (Hektor perished) Aeneas
              lives to reach Italy   Virgil keeps bees
        bones at rest   along the sea floor
              one like you are   one like I am
                   stella maris   prince of clowns

palace pavement   pissed on   vagrant
                              brethren   wearing skin
              am I not like you   ô man
                        am I not brother to man
        this very night afoot
                    through its patterned menace
                  falsity devised
            to be the antitestament to "and"
          pattern we inherit   of the palace we cannot

  I have found out its gate   have found out its door
                I have come into it

          what use guided me   hath vanished
    oath forsworn   gods pitiless
                  the pattern has its way

                                    paving stones
          devised to fascinate man's mind

though I walk I cannot think   nor remember
                      even my name or why I speak so

still   I have heard the nearer voice   the queerer voice
            have smelled him   have come upon his shit

              am I not brother equally to him
                              am I not freakish too
        mannish
                        but for my head

this our compact set   hasn't extension
      save   every separable
    marks the boundary
        the abutment
      the thrust

      so must
  imagination   measure
   what limits
     its love
against what today gave us   what
        took away

   let it stand
  nor bear against the hunter less   than greeting
 toward our meeting every step
     the taking hastens
  downward
   this declivity
   toward modest clay's unused "and"

what am I   that I am here   ô ye
    oddly copulated register of faith
  have you need of more than I have given
  are we not acquainted friends

 ô eve among the dated stones
   should I sleep beside them
    shall they whisper
      flesh
what went ye out for
  to see

angles made in transposition   long in ruins
    had I wandered

   through this tilting island's womb

innard streets   the Minos plan
that his wife become the mother of us all

the bull   sea pouring from his mouth

how many loves   bundle
                    misdirected obedience

          virile bull   none so white as he
translucid   had merely to mount
                              the king's wife
     to code the margin of time
                    the child has had only
                              to devour history

               how many loves
                         but none so unnatural
                                   as Pasiphaë

     conceived

how then shall the light be made suitable

          poet's breath   scarcely clouds the mirror
                         held to his lips
               translates fog   its swift massif   sea-gray
                    blowing across city's rooftop

                    night falls   all identities
                              fall with it

due immanenze
le double jeu
one stalking   one talking

of measures
for measures   weights   delays
the Minos bull's a pouring vase
whose stream
pools
in Libya's womb
pools again   in Europe's well
pools again
Pasiphaë

who shall deliver the name
we have realized the mixture of
down to the last of its series

left to heir it out
whispering "and"
forming the word with our lips

the incarnate world turns inside out
resembles air   spun
into white translucid thread
at the threshold
of breath

from *Hambone*

To My Father's Houses

◇　◇　◇

Each of you must have looked like hope to him
once at least however long it lasted
he who claimed he saw hope in every grim
eyeless gray farmhouse uninhabited
on a back road and hope surely was needed
every time they were shown into the bare
resonant rooms of the manse provided
by his next church and looked around to where
their lives would wake and they would never own
where they woke and he managed to buy you
never to live in though he thought he might
and projected you onto his days one
by one in the borrowed house they came to
for the last years until the sheet went white

from *The New York Review of Books*

Ashberries: Letters

◇　◇　◇

1.

Outside, in a country with no word
for *outside,* they cluster on trees,

red bunches. I looked up
ryabina, found *mountain ash.* No

mountains here, just these berries
cradled in yellow leaves.

When I rise, you fall asleep. *We
barely know each other,* you said

on the phone last night. Today, sun brushes
the wall like an empty canvas, voices

from outside drift into this room. I can't
translate—my words, frostbitten

fingers. I tell no one, how your hands
ghost over my back, letters I hold.

2.

Reading children's stories by Tolstoy,
Alyosha traces his index

over the alphabet his mouth so easily
unlocks. Every happy word resembles

every other, every unhappy word's
unhappy in its own way. Like apartments

at dusk. Having taken a different street
from the station, I was lost in minutes.

How to say, where's the street like this,
not this? Keys I'd cut for years coaxed open

no pursed lips. How to say, blind terror?
Sprint, lungburn, useless tongue? How say

thank you, muscular Soviet worker, fading
on billboard, for pointing me the way?

3.
Alyosha and I climbed trees to pick berries, leaves
almost as red. On ladders, we scattered

half on the ground, playing who could get them
down the other's shirt without their knowing.

Morning, the family gone, I ground the berries
to skin, sugared sour juices twice.

Even in tea they burned. In the yard,
leafpiles of fire. Cigarettes between teeth,

the old dvorniks rake, scratch the earth,
try to rid it of some persistent itch.

I turn the dial, it drags my finger back.
When the phone at last connects to you, I hear

only my own voice, crackle of the line.
The rakes scratch, flames hiss and tower.

4.
This morning, the trees bare. Ashberries
on long black branches. Winter. My teacher

says they sweeten with frost, each snow
a sugar. Each day's dark grows darker,

and streets go still, widen, like ice over lakes,
and words come slow to every chapped mouth,

not just my own, having downed a little vodka
and then some tea. Tomorrow I'll bend down

branches, brittle with cold, pluck what I can't
yet name, then jar the pulp and save the stones.

What to say? Love, I live for the letters
I must wait to open. They bear across

this land, where I find myself at a loss—
each word a wintering seed.

from *New England Review*

Trail

◇　◇　◇

prelude

　　　　this age our era i can correctly say this an era of exile
this satiny desert
on this trail of a thousand years there is us amidst misfits & assiduous trees

we have walked
over sand sick with evening of words spilling

　　　　　　　　what is the remedy for momentum for mania a deciduous heart?
loitering now i speak of nothing no ideas just việt nam motherland inside us
　　　　& between us the air　arizona sun magnanimous accepting everything

an ear of deaths in a polaroid photo & the killing
this age of hyper awareness this time of blue moons
　　　　　　of the year nineteen hundred ninety nine on the seventh day

　　　　　　　　　　the ocean　past we touch
　　　　　　　　　　　　inside our skin a sterling sound

we who have walked alone will no longer
through woods red with evening of dreams spilling
growing old a california sequoia green &
　　　　　　　　　sage as the saguaro branching

1

a crab crawls sideways into a polaroid photo tangled you loiter & now you speak of
nothing no ideas pushed into hole the fabric mice-chewed

you have been going back & forth from the border of . . . what was it?
when upon seeing a person with alzheimer's on tv when a flippant offer of someone
buying you something when after a family dinner in which the main conversation
was having desires versus shutting them off you wander into the streets eyes wet
while you notice how roseate the sky is how demure the heat is not its usual how you
should be enjoying such a night but nevertheless you go wherever your blind feet
take you places well-acquainted see cars pass & wonder if the headlights expose &
wonder if any will stop

2

wild-eyed
next to your border a different dialect spoken
                        in the corridor your fingers pressed

listening monk this laughing buddha belly & shoulders twitter a gurgle of ears listenin
pressed to palm
                                            when the mood strikes

            strike!
                                        when i begin
                        & drown in salt
                            the buddha's my own or lao tsze's in this mesme
        following the folds in robe

a boy dies saving another from suicide
on the suicide isle are mist gargantuan in deceptions

                words spilled the throat a babe on motorcycle rolls onto street

3

> to accelerate time i walk from arizona to texas to new york to
> việt nam
most content while making forgetting that night is night
> (rug   cat hair   crumb)

> & day day   this life is
to be in process is an act
> of survival
> follow the ends its awakened curves

through sterile passages of supermarkets i walk & walk
> to contend with time then suddenly lack
slowness   then speed   a velocity problem

a hyper awareness born of technology   a silver butterfly heavy

> inside this drift split

4

> "within 100 years of contact with western
> civilization, the amazon tribes become extinct"

news lurking
not even metal smithing nor the even-marking tires
the soles of defunct shoes
a blandness narrative can't obliterate

world news worsens these days
                       & you are not in my em-
           brace

        the axis spinning is why we don't fall off haunting earth
i haunt the earth
            looking
       for a phone this machine which allows us to be a-
                                      part
       how many digits is the number
                   for consciousness the total for God?

no one knows me wandering in this flesh
over the desert-feet soles of those i will never know
i am eager for the packed streets the embroiled pavements i wander in books finding
myself in paths that lead nowhere
                  but to designs in nature

i rove through strip malls grocery aisles of stuff cans & cans of songs looking loitering
& don't buy except
        what i need

                    (the everpresent Present the future it is here)
             a fault line the world grins
          & yet this hand full of epiphanies
                     minds that cannot escape nonchalance

5

(chiapas)

faces bought
from a witch doctor
carved stone of desolation
shrines to the past (it is here)

a high turn of sea of sun
                    & from this black jade survival

gone to the market fed there a life led there entrails bowls of bowels eaten
              meat meat & through stalls the tents striped with humor & flirtation

& men jerking off do you ever get sick of this?
                    they do it with a life's content
       of blossoms / ever the orange flowers drowning

see the spiders spinning caterpillars
                    sheets of blisters ricocheting off surf
                              aztec blood of zapatistas

6

not for the cantilever of arguments
nor the cumulus remarks
            the confused odor of tolerable american lives
nor the razor the vein nor for the contrapuntal snare do i come

but for the desert raging on a contact sheet the outbreak of pneumonia
                                    awkwardness of grand pianos
nonchalant pursuers of the dream the content hackers

i dream of sand dunes flying ridges & sun i dream of wind blowing darkly usurping
cultural designs   a liar in a tiger's den

in this city a blissful terror of invisible spires
cryptic skies talk less & less

                                    with my mother's hand
                                    i tether jade to the skin of books

shoring over names of friends who have left the last rite
i carve our faces on stone

                        ((disclose with a kayak in throat))

7

what noises are harbored in these chained boats?
sometimes these moments alone from wood pulp bleached

these thoughts

are belligerent
old women

i will be incoherent with them

8

my neighbors push
shopping
carts
home

9

amazonians on bare feet wooden dollies adorning their lips
women on new york streets high-heeled & aching

dreams of arizona: there are abscesses
    households trying to make ends meet

                                     dryness & trails
                in heat people come out at night like lizards
                          watch each other rodents slither
            the gila monster ecstatic

drawbridges dams impermeable we have our historical delusions try to live one day

10

              this soil of extremes
    a throb of mice in walls
                              assiduous trees a moon-shaped sickle
                                a dossier of stillness

see this aerial view
a body of shimmering water copies the blazing desert
water & some moon

                              twisted orifices of mountains
passing clouds shape of trees
waiting to see you i write this song on the plains
                  on spent mountains

try to sleep but words float up
what do animals do when they're alone?
they claw themselves till the blood flows (animals
                        we're fine in motion)

    this is what time does to you
          & clouds pass their leaves

          a snowflake fissured on window
                    patterned below the scandent mountains
        they've had a million years to practice their lines

                from *jubilat*

Behind the Orbits

◇   ◇   ◇

Queer ghost, whose aspect is focused backwards
mid-distance behind my gently closed eyes,
an increscent ill-drawn outline to view
that seems so like the softly filed concave
of her living face, I think it might speak,
relate, as did Antikleia, that day
last spent on the shore, the passive entry
into the salt-waves, the sift of wet sand
up through her warm feet, each footprint obscured
by the shifting mud until she is lost
from sight forever, enfolded within
the tidal force, the field of ceaseless stir.
Once there, the cartoon-view would first appear
as opalescent bubbles from a child's
toy plastic hoop, pea-green paddles of kelp
scallop around the strands of greenish hair
and flotsam seem like tiny forms of life
displaced by her shivering and weightless
form, airless air in a watery echo
of near-darkness, the gloom of that vista:
inverted sky, here and there cross-sectioned
by piercing columns of thick yellow sun;
at last her water-filled lungs will collapse
and she, relieved of grief, leave to await
her son in Hades, there where wingèd words
are coaxed by fresh spilt-blood; but while her life
was spun by Gods my immortal shadow

was by mortality impotent written
and thus is silent; no sweet wine, nor milk
nor barleycorn will spin the story out
from her dread-reft heart, she will weigh no more
synthetic choices, tonight it is I,
soul tapered slim by the lenient needs,
refined resolutions and dramatic *adieus,*
strung-out confessions of the pillow-side
conscience, who will mete out, the half-seas over
with guilt and longing, the humming verdict:
        "nothing can bring back the hour."
I did not say it, I could not think it,
worn out by three loitered years I gainsaid
the sentence, which indeed had from day-one
been dream-like. And then finally wasn't.
Now chords of nonsense words like cards unfold,
they clang in my ear. Unhappy their static
victory, a dry tongue in a spiritless
mouth, snapping foolish at every decree;
no time allowed to, head half-lifted, hear
the wind-drifts outside my window address
themselves to the half-broken trees, no time
for an ancient "footfall" to echo up
from beneath my thought; no time to push back
this coverlet and, in search of a guide,
walk through the wet ground to a sleep-drenched wood.
Custom must therefore provide my distinction,
as shades will still shake the dust from their feet,
dismiss our world and speak:
        Vacant I lay on the temporary cot
composing letters of regret *"My dear*
Brown, I should have had her when I was in health,"
I should have held her, I should have gone to her
though the truth at hand in her thinning glance
did not bear acknowledgment. Exit piety.
Enter love. And the compass will fashion
ephemeral harmony until some
felicitous "elsewhere" is stripped of its

comforting static and then the voices
will speak out again:
   "The earth is swiftly shovelled in"
the ground compressed, the vacuum of minutes
past in response and in horror, vivi-
sepulture, many nights I dreamt we had
performed the most precocious burial.
I checked the house before I left for fragments
of forgotten consequence, a piano
remained, a Windsor chair, a fold-down desk
with a broken hinge whose cubbies had been
thoughtlessly filled with: paper clips, pencils,
dry stamps and black coins, mechanical rig
for a manual mind to scratch near dry
a waterless leaf. Time was not trapped in
these things as I, who had loved their user,
would be, powdered dust from a liquid screen
setting the words of accomplishment free:
   "go not, like the quarry-slave in the night"
Stay, tell me of your life, as it is now,
as it was then, mollified rhetoric
of interstitial daylight, broken cup
on a peeling sill, where a hand, a will,
a mindless chore, a living cell-shred seized,
embraced, but so cold to the desperate
counterfeit kiss, the coward's unwitnessed
ritual. There is no eloquent grief.
It is not fit to outwit fate when heaven
has fallen upward, shoddy and garish
in its *streets of gold.* Flavorless metal,
hard to the teeth, ill-omened ore, folly-
sprung, root of the convex, bestial ears
that grew on the unwise King, whose servant
told the breeze that the breeze-stirred reeds might sing:
the life I denied the death of lies dormant,
different from what I supposed, and luckier.

from *Pressed Wafer*

Sympathy

◊ ◊ ◊

She's rubbing his shoulder
and he's reading about
Western birds. There's a scoop
of light just above my knee

it resembles the world, the one I know
a layer of smoke spread thin, a shelf

my mind returns again &
again to the picture
you gave me. In pain.
I'm holding the receiver
in Denver some woman making
human eyes at me from her
blue seat, but I later
conclude she's crazy

I'm helpless, rushing back to fix the
"h," how can I help you

I think we tried this long enough
our cure
we would save us from everybody
else, we "got" it,
us

and now we're another falling down car
complaining animal
empty house

you bleeding & expanding
until

the red night itself
is your endless disappointment
in me
who promised so much
on that hill.

O Glory to everybody & everything
that we will fish again & again
& get lucky

from *American Poetry Review*

Sunday Night

◇　◇　◇

Choose. If you want
meditation or poppy

or something altogether uncouth—
my riffle to your raffle

red façade to red façade
angel bucking sordid angel

Or why not make a malt of it? It's
virtually the same thing as a milkshake

but with powder. Powder is what's left
after the ideas have died. The sago palm

uncurls a new green hand into night. A truck
the size of Wisconsin drops off an acre

of rich mushroom compost in the yard
Let's get deep into it, make it our beard

Never fear, never fear, not while
the crescent moon is here, a crooked

smile of luminous jest. No matter what
happens next, remember this:

If a rice gets lonely, it will die.

from *The Hat*

Sonnet

◇ ◇ ◇

The tone poem left the door open.
Well, *close* it.
It doesn't stay. It reminds me of
Elizabethan plays where eyes,
especially the tragically blinded ones, are "jelly."
It has a center with a circumference loosely attached.
The ideas about social wastefulness
smeared over individual needs.

Since the ideas about wastefulness
are smeared over their objects,
the tone is everywhere.
It expresses its reluctance as virtue.
It is reluctant to intrude, like minds into
the fleetingness they concede.

from *Boston Review*

Haunt

◇   ◇   ◇

very facile, "Empty coffin"
The ground is blowing
Naked whistle
I'll just ask around the hotels
as to where I'm staying, the pale hotels
near the performance center
starting to emerge from the pollution.

anywhere you might chance it
though it's all the same except for death and perhaps another thing. is death a
discredited source
of information? is love for the dead discredited

I the painted giver of birth, the widow. again. Trying to experience texture of soul

Haunting the hospital

> dresses fabric ruin They need to know
>   this
> Walk over to a kind of danger
> an hour I go towards
> This was where I carried the bags
> of young snakes
> rue des Recollets dream
> Now to sit here not frightened
> Probably up there but it's not you
> in that room Make something change more
> Who
> There was no peace here, was there

No it was unhappiness, some neutrality When
When I slept   (Who)
I'm being him too
No one would want this information
Beautiful soul I or you   Countering
You don't have to say what
You didn't want to leave   Then spring
'I'm afraid I won't see it   I think I might really be dying'
'I think you might be too'
'That's why you're the one I can talk to'
Grass and the things in it
Why are you
I'm looking for poetry
it's here where it hurts us so much
I have to go on doing this
in a state of without   and that's why
I'm a transformer
Yes that's why

has been unfaithful in that bed that is has died and so I must leave him, how
it's rumpled where they were in the
afternoon if I leave him I will be self pictured as I am bereft the light a dim
blue in this very room emptied

    Need ceremony
    for
    change of luck
serpents hanging like cobwebs thin or swelling one might run from, don't
the poison of change
the poison of chance, then stay
in love of it   is that love
discredited? I need the power of all that's discredited,
I need things for my table of change luck
rip some silk off an orange scarf
and place it there
with pearls and a white gauze hospital mask
slips of paper on which are written the names of others I confuse him with
in my dreams, these items dreamed

and I must dream them again
that is, place them here in the poem to perform
        the ceremony
using what's discredited, a *list*
"kept her face" "used her face" that was I so place that face a
mask of stuck with the stuff sutures all of them black threads the heart it
burn I am calling to all bits of speech that apply to me
congregate in mass here to light in a small
holocaust, don't forget assessment in the ledger as "Terra Firma"
a woman's name, burn it.
the idea of the lost green jewels the theft the forfeiture, burn.
"certainty of style" burn that.
"wandering between deeds" burn
"she is stolen" burn
"I'm just trying to get some need"
"dédouaner" burn them
"half-naked, the shirt is black"
"the book blowing round like a doll" burn
"You just have to go through it" burn and burn
burn what everyone says of it
burn years and sequence
burn choice and burn proof
burn ". . . what are you frightened of"
burn the dead bird under green cloth
burn zero burn the idea of the universe
burn dreams
burn dreams
burn them as separate existence
burn all separation
burn all separation

now open open me to chance Really chance

                        from *Pharos*

Snapshot from Niagara

◇　◇　◇

We'd been married nine days,
the war had lasted a year,
we'd come to the falls
to photograph each other
with that roar behind us—

at dusk we asked an old man
to take a picture of us
embracing, but not too much—

how he fussed with the lenses
while we fumed: now, now,
while there's still light . . .

Already we resented each other
because we'd make us die
while alone we were immortal
like starlight or the breeze

and we were ashamed
never to have thanked him—
to be more lonely than ever
with a sheaf of glossy prints
of two dim faces, woman, man,
worn identical by happiness.

from *Barrow Street*

Frontis Nulla Fides

◇　◇　◇

Sometimes, now, I think of the back
of his head as a physiognomy,
blunt, rich with facial hair,
the elegant stone-wall shapes of the skull
like sensing features, as hard to read
as surfaces of the earth. He was
mysterious to me in his anterior depths,
occiput, lambdoid, but known like a loved
home outcrop of rock, and since words
can be lies, his silence had, for me,
a truthfulness, the preciousness of something
older than the human. I knew and did not
know his brain, and its woody mountain
casing, but the sheer familiarness
of his brow was like a kind of knowledge,
I had my favorite pores on its skin,
and the chaos, multiplicity, and
generousness of them was like
the massy stars over the desert.
And hair by hair the resolute shy
fiber creatures of his eyebrows—he hardly
frowned, he seemed serene, as if
above, or below, or alien
to anger. Now I can see that his eyes
were sometimes hopeless and furious,
but I saw them—and he seemed to feel them—
as lakes, one could sound them and receive no sense
of their bounds or beds. Something in
the paucity of his cheeks, the sunken

cheekbones, always touched me. Bold
ancient boner of the nose, wide
eloquent curve of the cupid's bow, its
quiver nearly empty, as if languagelessness
were a step up, in evolution,
from the chatter of consciousness. Now
that I travel the beloved land
of my husband's sealed mask of self
in memory, again, touching
his speechless contours—like the singing blind—
I feel that ignorant love gave me
a life. But from within my dream of him
I could not see him, or know him. I did not
have the art or there's no art
to find the mind's construction in the face:
he was a gentleman on whom I built
an absolute trust.

from *Ploughshares*

Twenty-six Fragments

◇　◇　◇

1.　　Music, that marvel
　　　trying to exist
　　　out of this forest to come forth

2.　　I find I am forgetting
　　　all the spoken　　　of
　　　and the numbers　　　(i.e.
　　　how to form them

　　　————————

　　　also the numbers

3.　　We don't really know what
　　　Reality is made of

4.　　In the play, the actors cry out
　　　But in the poem the words
　　　themselves cry out

5.　　Being with Mary: it has
　　　been almost too wonderful
　　　it is hard to believe

6.   I am not sure whether or not
I would like to live altogether
In the forest of poetry

Its mystery and its clarity

7.   I think I have written what I
set out to say—I need
not now turn to narrative

I have told not narrative, but
ourselves—no narrative but ourselves

8.
> I would speak of the world:
> I would speak for the world

9.   ~~Poetry must be~~

Clarity means, among
other things, to know
how the words come to meaning

to <u>experience</u> how the
words come to meaning

———————————

A note to Pound in heaven:

Only one mistake, Ezra!
You should have talked
to women

———————————

Poetry must be at least
as powerful as music, but
I am not sure that
it is possible

10. People visit, and I am
    shaken

11. Our little bird: I
    feel all my
    boyhood in
    him

12. **The world is black magic**
    The world is half magic

13. Bach: The B minor mass!
    I wept because it says
    everything that can
    ever be said

14. Once the singing was
    and is

15. We are entering a new era
    and nothing will be the same in the storm

    (written while that storm was
    blowing

    (post post modern)

16. The universe moved
    and we moved
    in this monstrosity

17a.　Cortez arrives.
　　　　　　　he is absolutely lost
　　　at an unknown shore.
　　　　　　　and he is enraptured

　　　(this is the nature of poetry

17b.　The poem:

　　　Cortez arrives at an unknown shore
　　　he is absolutely lost
　　　and he is enraptured

17c.　Cortez arrives at an unknown shore
　　　he is utterly lost
　　　but he is enraptured

18.　Rezi's last poems:
　　　just names, and the words
　　　themselves
　　　carry meaning　　　.　　　　somehow

19a.　These ordinary words
　　　　　　　come to mean
　　　　　　　everything

　　　In a way I live on words, forget words

19b.　The middle class boy to die
　　　in a foxhole like a
　　　dog

20.   Poetry is related to
        music and cadence and therefore to the
        force of events

21.   Hopkins   "my piece of being"

22.   Poetry is the word that comes to music

23.   The tamed ~~stones~~
        stones of the village

24.   Music: out of these
        houses to come forth

25.   tamed stones of ourselves

26.   The universe moved
        and *we* move
        In this monstrosity

                from *Facture*

JENA OSMAN

Starred Together

◊　◊　◊

A constellation of darkness
another of light

A gesture to be completed
by light
—CECILIA VICUÑA,
"Cruz del Sur"

A glance hits an object or person and pins it down like a star. The actual moves. Selective memory drama is what you experience, or is it what you see on the screen? While sitting in the box, images from a window are stolen from the street. The homes of the homeless become a story. The narrative drive is what clings to the actual moves; the narrative drive persists through the fragmentation in which seeing occurs. Juxtaposition in film is familiar. Even in soap operas. Piecing together the parts, the desolation alongside ("b/side") the pastoral garden. The washing of a pretty foot in the water of a hydrant. A beautiful woman resting in a garden in a white lace "shift." The blue tarps spread over the makeshift houses. You have a bird's eye view. Shifting from one response to another. Laughter in the garden makes itself so. Without a home, inspired (defeated?) by what has disappeared completely. Trying to avoid that which you'd like to disappear, and yet, no matter how you focus your lens, it strikes you again and again. Shift away for the view, and your self is drawn in on rip tide. The sound of the bulldozers as they sweep the yard clean. The waves of debris float forward to the edge of the earth. You look through the trees into the garden to see a space that is unified. The perversion of your own observation as it crawls towards summary.

The position of the stars determines your character. Stolen from a window on Wall Street, the bathroom of a bordello. Slit down the middle vertically. All the bodies and narratives divided into a split screen. We peer and see money, clothing, skin. Substances exchange. You think it's from your childhood, but see it later on video as happening long before your childhood. At the bottom of the window, facing away from you, is a mirror—thus each of the room's occupants face the mirror and in turn (unknowingly) face you. Seeing what's not supposed to be seen. Seeing others see themselves. "Voyeur?—C'est Moi!" More so than when you sat in the box and a woman whom you have been following (as in narrative) stares back at you. But the circumstance of looking has fewer ramifications—can realizing the corruption of your own detached look, in response to this place, cause anything to happen? Can realizing the corruption of your own detached look—in the face of the other place, in walking down the street without seeing—cause anything to happen? You see yourself looking and trust that it is enough.

A systematic assemblage: the Pleiades. The means by which people who have nothing, make something of it. You follow one particular shack and watch it transform from owner to owner. Architecture and interior design as representative of an identity and position. First there is a roof. Then there is a door. Then there is a fake address, because numbers mean nothing here against a stone building in Chinatown. You are no longer looking at yourself looking. Instead, inspecting what someone has made in the face of a city's refusal. The object of your gaze is no longer a figure that you follow (as in narrative). The objects become subjects in the fact of their creations, and so resist your self-reflection. They show you their houses and the procedures of their being there at all communicate the occupants, not you. Can looking save? When you look at a constellation, you draw the points together with your own lines. But when someone catches your eye in a direct grip, there are no more stars. You might shake your hands at the sky as the light crashes in, we're pinning you down. You might shake your head to clear it, then step inside.

from *Hambone*

Fretwork

◊ ◊ ◊

Reports are various—
conflicting also:

many fell,
       a few;

like taken cities. . . .

★

Whether or not
to any loss there is weight
assignable,

              or a music given

—some play of notes,
slow-trumpeted,

for which to listen
is already to be
too late;

              whether forgetting is
or is not proof of
mercy, henceforth let

others say.

★

Is not victory itself
the proof of victory?

★

Little hammer, chasing—onto
unmarked metal—pattern,
decoration,

a name,

a scar upon the face
of history, what

has no face

★

Of briar
and thorn, my bed.

★

—I stand in clover.

from *The Threepenny Review*

"A roof is no guarantee . . ."

◇ ◇ ◇

★ ★ ★

A roof is no guarantee
that you'll sleep

The unease of premises
pins together the curtains
at night

Waiting for a clearness
of purpose

Eating 3 meals a day
We go to bed hungry

Privacy is not a remedy

We've become separated
by "efficiencies"
Nobody can do anything with

A kind of machine person
Floundering in the dark

It's hard to believe
5 sparrows were sold for this

from *Chicago Review*

ADRIENNE RICH

Ends of the Earth

◇　◇　◇

All that can be unknown is stored in the black screen of a
    broken television set.
Coarse-frosted karst crumbling as foam, eel eyes piercing
    the rivers.
Dark or light, leaving or landfall, male or female demarcations dissolve
into the O of time and solitude. I found here: no inter/
ruption to a version of earth so abandoned and abandoning
I read it my own acedia lashed by the winds
questing shredmeal toward the Great Plains, that ocean. My
    fear.

Call it Galisteo but that's not the name of what happened
    here.

If indoors in an eyeflash (perhaps) I caught the gazer of spaces
lighting the two wax candles in black iron holders
against the white wall after work and after dark
but never saw the hand

how inhale the faint mist of another's gazing, pacing, dozing
words muttered aloud in utter silence, gesture unaware
thought that has suffered and borne itself to the ends of
    the earth
web agitating between my life and another's?
Other whose bed I have shared but never at once together?

from *American Poetry Review*

CORINNE ROBINS

Les Demoiselles d'Avignon

◇ ◇ ◇

After Picasso

Posed for our waiting customers,
blue lights and pinkest skin,
love is war as we group together
before the table, the fruit,
our secret slit—
Come, taste our perfumed sweat!
nudes with carved masks,
with five pairs of mismatched eyes
ugly and beauty equally sexy
looking to see you.
One nude sitting back to front,
with monstrous mask,
an African medicine to cure your sickness
here among bodies like rebuilt dreams,
a single hand, five fingers
flattened holding the wall
where love is war for witches
locked up in houses,
elegances of skin out of the sun—
oh bleed for us,
who have the last laugh,
on that street in Barcelona—

We demoiselles,
behind and in front of heavy curtains,
the painted images of Fernande and Laurencin

line up, arms behind—
taste our perfumed sweat,
as mothers of men's fantasies
against sky-blue stare out
singing of Avignon, of a canvas circus,
of statuesque statues,
threatening as a room of welcoming women
who would and would not be tamed
lest the dog jump too high—
lest you fear all of us pretty ones
lurking in front of blue and red lights,
with those masks, those striving eyes,

where from that bordello,
bordello is a more mellow word—
for that jungle of fear behind
those walls, unpacked from a box
the painted sum of his destructions
stand with distorted mouths,
posed for camera, for brush
bodies turned inside out
to ask who threatens you.
—Dark animals standing
as if lying down,
sharp angled giantesses, brazen-faced
with staring eyes challenge;
we, a small man's love,
we five, the world's evil eye,
demoiselles of a murderous race—
other, other, and of that secret mirror,
the feminine, with pursed mouths
summon you.

from *Talisman*

ELIZABETH ROBINSON

Tenets of Roots and Trouble

◊   ◊   ◊

This begins the chapter pronounced "creation."
> Here speaks a purple tissue
> fulminated.
> Organ, not alive, but somewhat

> upward, yeasty from the growing rift.

Pursues contrast with trust in its forbearance.

★

Foretold by weeping
> lined with a green and ragged border.
> > The will to go back, later, interpolate narrative.
> > Exhume the lists.

> > > This mission announces birth, despite our defunct
oral history.
> > You have seen, edged
> > > with serrated leaves.
> > Not derivative, but hemmed in
by the mouth. She yawns.

Prior to the fruit of the shade, I leave with you,
> journey as bequest.

It says in reference
> "intermittent"
> > as a hope stenciled on the coming proof.

★

All things in common.
               Metaphorically
               feet.
        Simulate the ingestion of
           face, extremities.
        Yes, hands, toes become the absolutes.

    Such friable biology
              unconvinced in the reconciler.

        All of whom believed together by repetition.

Drowsy, amiable absence
      whose plenty resides in alias.
      Ridiculous.
           Noted the meat of the crop inching up from soil
           and emulated its captive love of flesh.

All claims for overflow being, *prima facie,* equivalent.

★

Give kisses to the least reliable,
          or backtrack to capitalize
          letters, even nouns.

            Kiss them
        as indefinite.
            The risk
        like a fragrance.
            At least one
        of us, offering, should lean forward.

Juice as synonym:
        Five tidbits doled out like lemon on the tongue.

May your enemies partake with you of the stars
        though you preserve the rind and fat
for yourselves.

In pursuit
        may all sourness become pleasurable.
Foresee the urge—
        what is tedious made luxury.

Wrung out of the drinking rag, common to all.

★

Cross as anagram for succor and soreness;
        vowelless alphabet whom all refuse to approximate.

    Cross as intersection abetted by disguise.
        Tables turned:
        detritus of any launch is the landing pad.

Debts grow roots.
        Simple declarative: I tug

        the stem. Loam and little fear
        bared to the sun.

Little do we know the grace of the measure;
pray each night that our needs and calloused

        knees not be forgiven.

    Another interest collects. Homophonous and literal dew.

★

Piecemeal, fragmentation's cement.
        Or, lost in prepositions,
        the palsied hand
        lifts a spoon of broth.

To be a peace is to be partial; spill.
   Where is the mouth for which our personified
      spoon aims.
   Old, broken, spastic hand,
      relay hope to my tongue.
            Quick-descending link, this soupy air.

There was a tribe adopted first person singular pronoun:
                  I.

I am.
I am beast, bird.
I am mourning

the failure of the name, a solid wall, like that
            in Jericho,
            wavering under the blight, those trumpeters.

Only meant to scold,
            not raise options.
            Fused. So celestially willful.

★

Little head pressed in the cleft between breasts.
            Brief glimpse.
            Divinatory cowlick.

            The hour decays—sugar in lumps
            softens, sand-like.

This is a discrete future which does make promises,
            breathing one vow into another.

                  Tooth
         pushing up through the gums.

from *Hambone*

IRA SADOFF

Self-Portrait with Critic

◇　◇　◇

One idiot took me for a Vietnam vet.
"You have that tattooed damaged look."

Other descriptions? Jaded, pent-up,
wrathful, loyal, swerving toward hysteria.

Anyway, that's how she put me together.
She was a polyp in the clandestine tale

of what holes we are, what a factory
of piecework, stitched together

with bad wardrobes and bartered expressions.
To look at me, I hurt seems past tense,

synthesized into a gaze that drifts toward stable.
But passing is nobody's business, who you are

is a secret to everyone, that's American
as being an exception, believing in

your own invention, tinkering around
in a minor key, since no one's listening.

And inside, let's not make it pretty,
let's save the off-rhyme and onomatopoeia

for the concert hall, let's go to the wormy place
where the problematic stirs inside his head,

something's jumbled inside the cells,
something chemical sticking to the walls

where the doctor looks down your throat,
down the tunnel where you sleep and wash up,

where you can't get over how dogs spar
with their masters, how Contras could tear

a newspaper in two and then bury the nuns.
Anyway, you can see how a sentence

might tear the heart out of someone,
closing in on and looking down at the mess

from some trim square of property
that's busily employed and invested

in making things work, with an ardor
and intensity that slips away into the ethereal,

all the while reciting some butchered version
of *The Ancient Mariner,* humming in your head

The Pavanne for a Dead Princess,
because you lean toward the luxurious,

the artful, the second-hand, once-removed.

from *AGNI*

I Do Not Know Myself

◇ ◇ ◇

I do not know myself
I go to dark and am of dark

Ignorant of myself

I sleep and dream—
But not enlightened

Nor when I wake
And remember dream

All I have not seen
All I will not see again

That I will take to ignorant dark

Desire is unchanged
Year on year it is on

Each page to turn
Each face to love

If I lived
Till the end of the world

It would never be done

Once I was a son
Once I had all the time in the world

Now a day starts
Now it ends
Now a window is dark

from *Poetry*

You Also, Nightingale

◇　◇　◇

Petrarch dreams of pebbles
on the tongue, he loves me
at a distance, black polished stone
skipping the lake that swallows

worn-down words, a kind of drown
and drench and quench and very kind
to what I would've said. Light marries
water and what else (unfit

for drinking purposes), light lavishes
my skin on intermittent sun. (I am weather
and unreasonable, out of all
season. Petrarch loves my lies

of laurel leaves, ripped sprigs of
deciduous evergreen.) A creek is lying
in my cement-walled bed, slurring
through the center of small

town; the current's brown and
turbid (muddy, turbulent
with recent torrents), silt rushing
toward the reservoir. A Sonata

passes by too close (I have to jump)
and yes I do hear music here. It's blue, or
turquoise, aquamarine, some synonym
on wheels, note down that note. It's Petrarch

singing with his back to me (delivering
himself to voice), his fingers
filled with jonquil, daffodils, mistaken
narcissus. (I surprised him

between the pages of a book,
looked up the flowers I misnamed.)
Forsythia and magnolia bring me
spring, when he walks into the house

he has wings. Song is a temporary thing
(attempt), he wants to own his music.

from *New England Review*

For Larry Eigner, Silent

◇　◇　◇

Our endless yawp
The poem is a field of action
　　　　　　pigeons
　　　　　　　　roosting in the eaves
　　　　　　of the concrete train station
　　　blink with intention
The lights at any intersection
at night change colors
regardless of the traffic
In the basement a pipe
drips quietly
into the waiting bucket

Moon in the poplar tangled
sets just before the sun
first rising throws shadows
the way a ventriloquist does voices
long, lean, stretching back into compactness
Light then we realize is just an illusion
Real-time, thick as any oatmeal, twisted
coagulates intention
　　　　　　　　Baboon
will fight a crocodile
if it's grabbed an infant

Behind me,
where the hospital corridor should be,
I find a street corner

around which a klezmer band is marching
approaching yet never arrives

Whom should I notify first?
The term "intention" returns
in the guise of will, would
hard grained, knotted
thru which surface any day now
the first green shoots of a new year
vulnerable to the frost will bloom

Find in the counsel of dreams an old tune
the band itself half forgotten
beneath the shards of melody
to locate a tone
as an index to emotions
not recognized at the time but held
closely, more so than that to which we thought we'd paid attention

A quality of light underneath the streetlamp
is how it dampens color
how color itself is a thing imposed
as the sun imposes day

Day, when it arrives
if it arrives, is layered
and must be stripped
although never in the same way twice
if ever we are to discover
the pulse at the core

What fiction, what nonsense

Voices over in the corner, jabbering
with no thought of who listens

2.

The line already is inherent in the upright letter, oriented. Speech is not
a given. The tongue is infected. It is very cold. Worlds hurtle through the

night sky, where it is apparent that day is the exception, that it may even be a fiction, a creation not of light, but of desire. I WANT SPEECH. Sky, air, wind, sun surround. For want of storm windows, we hung quilts. Birds shake snow from the lighter branches. The traction faction. One doesn't so much sleep under all these blankets as one does cook. Pencil is a blunt instrument. In a coma, I am told, all evidence of palsy disappears, you yawn freely, widely, the way an infant yawns asleep. I shall not hear birds in these trees again. Words hurtle through the night sky.

3.

Stripped of furnishings, the familiar house became exactly what it was: an object, alien, a machine, each room a potential or function. There, in the leafless forest, we could see the huge nest high atop a poplar. From here I can walk to the train, so much assumed in the instant, twenty-five bones per hand or foot, three muscles roughly for every bone. Behind that wall, the low hum of the furnace. After several days of warmer temperatures, the snow still has not melted, the last mounds dark and translucent, cakes of ice. Odd how, after 30 years, a phrase such as "the beauty wapiti" still rings in the mind. Oncoming cars' headlights shimmer dimly in the fog. At the road's edge, back in the trees, the deer watch us, witness without interpretation. The flower's knowledge of its own process is not counted as mind. I walk with each hand balled into a fist.

4.

"Oh yeah
    you're

        one of the ones

        who can
            write in the dark"

        from *Facture*

Poem after Haniel Long

◇ ◇ ◇

Morning and nothing
again I beseech thee, my king,
as the space disappears in the light
against curls of clouds
dawn keens under the blue sky dome
prison of my gaze and walls
my voice as the flesh my soul.
I put forth my sins
into earth and atmosphere
to call my Lord's light
through this region of waste
where last night under flame
chills eased at my touch
and the cold death of a man
warmed under my palms.
Shamed, I am lord to these
ungoverned races, their sickness and poverty
my salvation and trade.
That we should be made
of limp wet meat
appears strange to me
as that we should be also
air and spirit
in these hours when nausea
follows a quick curiosity. . . .

Several years passed
before I could relax
in that living plexus

for which even now
I have no name;
but only when at last
I relaxed could I see
the possibilities of a life
in which to be deprived of Europe
was not to be deprived of much.

Tribe after tribe,
language after language
who could recall them all?
They robbed and
        lost their only goods
    on our way onward
        trading rest and food
at great discomfort.

Moonlight in another adobe village
bellies globed on frames
and each so hungered
delirium rang the ears
keeping up for hours the naked flash
from center to periphery,
and back again.

Once it rained
and in that dusk we met
women in an opening.
They took us to be gods
floating in the mist
and led us to a village
of fifty huts.
There we cured and cured. . . .

from *Mungo vs. Ranger*

GUSTAF SOBIN

In Way of Introduction

◊ ◊ ◊

poems are about. yours, though,
yours, it would seem, are
a-
bout the process of their own
depletion: about, one might assume, the sheer a-

boutlessness of being, oh nexus of
nobody's, *nulla* in the knotted
musculature of
its

very mirrors: is what, vaporous, the lids would
with-
hold; seal, if only they
could, beneath the coil of their

clamped lashes. tell, tell the tongue, then, to
its shadows; the
long-

boned breath to those troughed
chaotic landscapes
of
linen. for here, here's what we'd wrought to its

very

effacement. oh blown
effigy, what matters, finally, isn't to be written.

from *Hambone*

JULIANA SPAHR

Some of We and the Land
That Was Never Ours

◇   ◇   ◇

Note: Someone was singing we are all in this world together. There were some grapes. Someone was feeding sparrows, making them perch on the thumb and eat out of the hand if they wanted any food. The sparrows preferred to eat on the ground. In memory there was a story of a French grandfather who left early in my father's life, moved to Canada, and died by falling off a horse. We were tourists. There were long lines. My mother waited in them. I sat outside and took notes. I thought about the vines that grew in France, then came as cuttings to California, then went back to France after a blight. I thought about who owned what. And divisions. And songs sung in bars. And inaugural poems. I was trying to figure out a day. I came home and used a translation machine to push these back and forth. The versions of the exchange are on the left. First and final English versions are combined on the right. Things are edited slightly.

1

We are all. We of all the small ones are. We are all. We of all the small ones are. We are in this world. We are in this world. We are together. We are together. And some of we are eating grapes. Some of we are all eating grapes. Some of we are all eating. We are all in this world today. Some of we are eating grapes today in this world. And some of we let ourselves eat grapes. In the eating of grapes. We of all the small ones are what eats grapes. In the world of grapes. Eating grapes. We of all the small ones are what eats. Some of we are all together in the grapes. We of all the small ones are today in this world. In this world. By eating grapes. To eat grapes.

Some of we let ourselves eat grapes today in this world. Some of we let ourselves be all together in the grapes. In the world of the grapes. In this world. In grapes. In the grapes. In taste. In the taste. In fermentation. In the fermentation. In wine. Out of the wine. In fresh tight skin. In the fresh tight skin. In seed. Out of seed. In moisture. In the moisture. In today. In the today. We are all in this world together. We of all the small ones are together in this world. In the we are all together. In we let ourselves be all together. Some of we are eating. Some of we let ourselves eat. Some of we are all together eating grapes. Some of we let ourselves be all the grapes to be eaten together. This place. In this place. In the eating. While eating. In the grapes some of we are all eating. In all the undeniable grapes of we let us leave itself let ourselves be what eats. In the eating of grapes. By eating grapes. We are all today. We of all the small ones are today. The grapes in the eating. In the we are. In the are. In the grapes are. Eating grapes. In the we the world. In the together. Some of we are all in this world together eating grapes.

2

Some of we and the land that was never ours while we were the land's. Started from us and of the ground which was never with we while we were the ground. Some of we wore the land. Some of we carried the ground. Some of we planted grapes. Some of we were to settle. Some of we were to arrange. And the land was never ours. And the ground was never with us. And yet we were made by the land, by the grapes. We were made by the ground, by the grapes. We were eating the leaves of the land. We ate the sheets of the ground. The grapes of the land. Grapes of the ground. The green of the land. Green of the ground. The leaves. Sheets. And we were the land's because we were eating and the land let some of us eat. And we were the ground because we eat and the ground let some among us eat. And yet the land was never some of ours. But the ground was never sure with us. Is never some of ours. Be never certain with us. Never will be rightly some of ours. Be correctly never certain with us. Never to be owned. Never to be had. And the land's green is the land's owning of us. And the green of the ground is the possession of the ground of us.

3

The land is some of us holding out our hand and sparrows are pecking at it eating. The ground is among us giving out hand and the sparrows picotent with it eating. We are all in this world, this world of hands and grain, together. We all the small ones are in this world, this world of the hands and grain, together. Some of us are sparrows pecking at our hand. Some among us are sparrows picotant with our hand. Flying then nesting on our finger. With then control the hardware on our finger. Sparrows are pecking at our hand, pecking at our grain, at our hand, at our grain, at our hand. The sparrows picotent with our hand, picotant with our grain, our hand, our grain, our hand. We are all in this world with sparrows. We all the small ones are in this world with sparrows. With pecking. With the picoter. We are in this hand, in this pecking. We are in this hand, in this picoter. We are all. We all the small ones are. Some of we are pecking back. Some of we let ourselves picotons behind. We are pecking at our hand. We picotons with our hand. We are wanting to be full with grain. We want to be full with the grain. And then to be eating grapes. And to eat grapes then. Some of we are flying at our hand, flying at our hand. Some of we let ourselves fly to our hand, rollings up with our hand. Some of we are pecking at our hand of flying. Some of we let ourselves picotons with our hand of the flight. We are all in this world together, flying pecking. We all the small ones are together in this world, controlling the picoter. Down on the ground. With bottom on the ground. Then again, flying, pecking. The other side, to fly, picotant.

4

What it means to settle. What means it arrangement. To we are all in this world together. We all the small ones are together in this world. To eat the grapes and not to plant the seed. To eat the grapes and not to plant seed. To hold on too tight. To be too strongly held in the function. To change. To change. To make the change. To make the change. To change the land. To change the ground. To throw out the seed. To throw out of seed. To we are all in this world together yet still some of we are eating grapes, others pecking at the hand. We all the small ones are together in this world always however that some of us eat grapes, others which picotent with the hand. How to move. How to move. How to move from settle on top to inside. How to move stabilization on the top inside. To embrace, to not settle. To embrace, not to arrange. To speak. To speak. To spoke. With the spoke. To poke away at what it is that is wrong in this world we are all in together. To push far what is with it is incorrect in this world which all the small ones are us in the unit.

from *Chicago Review*

JOHN TAGGART

Call

◇   ◇   ◇

In what memory as a stream carries along
and without announcement
announces

a sort of resurfacing
coming up to the surface of what is not memory

in the middle of memory and habit
out of memory and habit and desire in the middle of the day

and not a matter of words and thus almost frightening
as what announces without announcement
is frightening

slightest ripple slightest swirl
no more than a moment a moment of silence over the
telephone
as the cards say
of "deepest sympathy."

from *The Café Review*

from Raton Rex, Part I

◊   ◊   ◊

An island is an "o" with
a slash across it in Danish
but an island nevertheless
to ride in a cab on a crooked
beam of it with 3 women
in the back seat me with
driver in front watching
out the windshield the rows
of houses & buildings
to Wooster Street in SoHo
you begin to feel life
though still curiously not
alive per se the way you
would if you were a tree
I wish that I could speak
of some agony observing
the decapitation. Fiery streams
batter the fuselage. I watch
ants that have found a way
in through a seam in
the window frame one by
one emerge following the
corner of the wall to climb
on my letters. I don't know how
to say this except to say
there is a cockroach living in
my computer. A woman sat
beside me & I observed
her cleavage. Drops of blood

Wipe the back of my hand
across my mouth. I taste
leaves. I feel funny. My
back hurts. My head is
still attached to it. I want
air, space, a column
sunshine, laughter & this
is no joke when you see
how much what we do
costs in terms of money
which are calories which are
units of heat first in light
of the sun which is God's
money converted into

potential a candle's glow
which you can't have with-
out the thought of its being
snuffed plunged into
darkness. Darkness
is a privilege which is what
you find at a city's center
or edge if you can find
it like in Connemara
but to speak of the hard
flat-devoured plains is
difficult as it is to find
the heart also in the city
I mean where I mean
where do we place the bomb
if it were one that
when it explodes would
become the shards of
life as we know it here
on this uncharted desert
island in the sense of
which is the epitome
of city life to feel one is
Crusoe cruising the canyons
ferreting out from niches

bits of useful fauna
& scaring up ground animals
or snaring birds handing
money your life in
your hands over to
clerks behind glassed-in
partitions who are the
tutelary spirits of this
island, benign kind exacting
intermediaries of our
conditional survival
propitiations to whom
are necessary to get
choice beef slices

Slowly it has come to pass
that the sky is an irregular column
of truth through which
whiz insects, zephyrs
distinct impressions
the Rorschach of which
are seen in the clouds
which curiously I don't
spend much time reading
anymore having come
into closer communion
with antipodes luminous
& vast as are these senses
portals of taste of touch of
lying beside my brown-
skinned woman in the
morning as the day
hard at first & green
ripens into a perfected
sphere on the surface of
which may be discerned
in order the punch-list
timetable the invoice &
ladling order possessed of
which humanity has come

to be inside & out
washed out. Namely
I don't know when life ceased
to touch me & came
instead to cut right through
this chasm that I span
in me this circle
of effects that defines
a center a hole through
which I consume what
defines & holds in place
Sam a state of hands

from *Boston Review*

JEAN VALENTINE

Do flies remember us

◇ ◇ ◇

Do files remember us
We don't them
we say "fly"

say
"woman"
"man"

you   gone
through my hands
me through your hands

our footprints feeling
over us
thirstily

from *Colorado Review*

Eye Contact

◇　◇　◇

We make eye contact across the crowded room
    but I'm too tired to speak

I write her a letter but at the last minute
    decide not to mail it

She writes in her diary how much she hates me—
    I shouldn't have read it

The Trojan War was a play put on for the pleasure
    of the gods

The Trojan War was produced by Zeus for his own pleasure

Deficient kidneys are often due to excessive loss of semen

Economic growth is promoted at the direct expense
    of human health

I saw you walking towards me from a distance but I lowered
    my eyes when we passed & you didn't say anything,
    you didn't say anything

The last time I saw her she was crossing Canal Street
    with her baby

Hold firmly to your goals, remain flexible in your methods

We met at a party & spent the next week in bed

We met at a bar, she told me her life story, & we never
    saw each other again

Every night, after the play, he gave the key to his motel room
    to a different guy

Heard the one about the woman who left her car running
    while she went to the store & when she came back
    the car was gone, & her baby

Heard the one about the affluent teenagers who murdered
    their baby

You risk everything without thinking of the future
    or what you can gain

It's possible to take a risk, for its own sake, & not go crazy

You can speculate with the hope of gaining something
    which doesn't exist

"What you spit out falls back on you"—I copied that
    from a book

I copied some lines from Nietzsche & quoted them back to you
    but you weren't interested

I tried to impress her with my knowledge of Nietzsche, but
    she wasn't interested

They say you can't be happy unless you learn to forget
    but I remember every word everyone said, every time
    someone said something intentionally to hurt my
    feelings, or to retaliate for something I did

I begin telling her my problems but she interrupts me
    mid-sentence

He pulled the ski-mask over his head & told the woman
    in the grocery to hand over her money

He threatened to kill the woman in the grocery if she didn't
    give him the money

We come from Korea, open a grocery, work our asses off—
    & look what happens

One day a guy with a ski-mask & a gun came into the store
    & asked for money, but I didn't give it to him

I used to go to parties, sit in the corner, & wait
    for someone to talk to me

The body of the Korean woman was discovered behind the
    counter of her grocery

The teacher who was molested in the stairwell identified
    her attacker through a 1-way mirror

It's possible if you go to bed with your teacher you'll learn
    more than if you sit in a class with your hands folded:
    may I leave the room?

The student asked the teacher for permission to go
    to the bathroom & never returned

I stare at the woman across from me in the subway
    car but when she looks up from her book
    I turn away

It's one thing—to be aggressive—to go after what
    you think you want—& another thing—to sit back
    & wait for something to happen

The guy in the car behind me honks his horn
    because I'm going too slow

All I ever wanted to do was come to this country
    & open a grocery

The dog follows the scent of the animal into the clearing

We track down animals, skin them alive, & sell them
　　to people who are hungry

I told the psychiatrist at the army inductee center
　　that I didn't like women, & he believed me

A woman props her elbows on a cushion behind a screen

No one is to blame for your suffering but yourself

You can stand up, in the vertical position, until your head
　　hovers above the skyline, or lie in your suburban
　　sweat box until the branches begin to sway

We were two solitaries, eating alone in a crowded restaurant,
　　staring at one another covertly above our plates

Even my words, now, this, copied from my own notebook,
　　something someone else said, can't write her name
　　without regret

She asked me what my intentions were, & I said: let's be
　　friends

Sometimes it's best to be friends with someone, before falling
　　in love

I go outside with a gun in my pocket like a *petit bourgeois*

They were loading their groceries into the back of their
　　station wagon when a guy with a ski-mask came up behind
　　them & demanded their money

We met outside K-Mart & went for a coffee at Starbucks

Peyote poison presents symptoms similar to polio

Physical beauty & bodily health reflect good character

Because a lot of people say something, it must be right

Friendship is a response to the tragedy of love

Once the longing for a new world & for the tree of life
    seizes the heart, who knows what may come next

I can hear the sound of my voice saying something
    I already said

I stop to catch my breath where the road turns uphill

Resemblances proliferate in a swarm of analogies

The cop who stopped me for speeding wiped the sweat
    from his chin

from *The Hat*

Return to Saint Odilienberg, Easter 2000

◊   ◊   ◊

At the mouth
of a minor tributary
winding about a man-made hill,
rises the church, its two towers
like teeth. At its feet my parents lie
tucked under river stones
that she assembled there to cover him
then she too slipped in
pulling the coverlet up to her chin.

Years go by, time growing thin.
The bells ring distantly.
I hear them tug at me and bring
my own descendants there
to be aware of roots. They bring
bluebells picked in the meadows
left on the stony hearts
of those who built me.

Then the doors fly open
when Christ rises. In the dark
apse red blazes like blood.
Here all the cherubim assembled
sing me back, a child the age
of those I brought from far to hear
what I heard then, AGNUS DEI.

Trumpets are announcing
a future still intact
with alleluias. How improbably
eternal is the need to resurrect
past knitted into future,
the world wrapped in a river,
the children and the dead.

from *Witness*

In Charge

◇ ◇ ◇

"I collect dogs. What of it?
It's like collecting sky
you got to go out every day.
See the kid who just fell
over the guy's bottle?
One dog and he ties it
around everybody's legs.
Hey Pudsy, come over here darling.
Trisha, leave him alone.
Trisha's got a sore on her back
and it bothers people.
When I got my first
they said it would help
meet someone but with 16 dogs
I don't need anybody.
Don't touch that, *Kumquat.*
The whole park knows me but nobody
knows me. You'd have to be a dog.
There's no responsibility
because they've each got 15 friends.
I'm just in charge. *Landon,*
come on. We're going over there."

from *Hanging Loose*

Illumined with the Light
of Fitfully Burning Censers

◇   ◇   ◇

Intelligent voice of a suburban housewife,
Present & accounted for, sir.
Really got a good deal on those filters,
On that service, on these curtains, really
Got a good parking place, good appointment
With the orthodontist, with the guidance
Counselor, really did well with the raffle
Tickets, with the ceviche and raisin salad,
Got a really good parking place, finished
That coffee off in a hurry, got a really
Good deal with that housekeeper, her husband
Wants to do yardwork as well, got a really
Good deal with the babysitter her mother's
A seamstress on the side. On the side of
What, did not ask. Got a really good deal
On napkins, felt good about their color, got
An okay parking place, did pretty well with
The birdseed, got a great deal on the flag-
Stone, really found a decent way to get out
Of the committee work, wrote seven thank-
You notes, sent flowers quite easily, got
A really good parking place, made an excel-
Lent cob salad, found a shortcut to the
Fishmarket, remembered the fishmonger's name,
Remembered to pick up the dry cleaning, to
Pass by the wine shop, got an okay parking place,

Checked into fall schedules, got a perfect
Appointment with the accountant, made real
Headway with the holiday schedule, found the
Perfect gift for my sister, remembered to
Check at the postoffice for the missing
Delivery, noticed the new postal rates, looked
At the wanted posters, went to the bank, spoke
With the teller about foreign currency, saw
Myself on the telemonitor, looked up a recipe
For buffalo, got a lousy parking space, felt
Really good about everything that got done
Today, picked up a magazine, said no to a
Solicitor, placed an order, checked on the
Buffalo, read a book by Ed Hirsch, dreamed
He was my wife.

from *Volt*

Nostalgia II

◇ ◇ ◇

January, moth month,
                    crisp frost-flank and fluttering,
Verona,
Piazza Bra in the cut-light,
                    late afternoon, midwinter,
1959,
Roman arena in close-up tonsured and monk robed
After the snowfall.

Behind my back, down via Mazzini, the bookstore
And long wooden table in whose drawer
Harold will show me, in a month or so,
                    the small books
From Vanni Scheiwiller, *All'insegna del pesce d'oro,*
That will change my life,
Facsimiles, *A Lume Spento,* and *Thrones,* full-blown, in boards.

Made in Verona. Stamperia Valdonega.
That's how it all began, in my case,
                    Harold and I
Ghosting the bookstores and bars,
Looking for language and a place to stand that fit us,
The future, like Dostoyevsky, poised
To read us the riot act.
                    And it did. And it's been okay.

from *Ploughshares*

A Sheath of Pleasant Voices

◇　◇　◇

There are rooftops
made of cloud remnants

gathered by a trader
dabbling in car parts and burlap

At night, I dive onto the breeze
fermenting above the dirt

and dream that I am a crocodile
a tin of shoe polish, an audience of two

In the morning, before the smallest yawn
becomes a noodle, I am offered

a ribbon of dense yellow smoke
I opt for fuzzy rocks and clawed water

and, of course, the perishable window
I am one of the last

computer chain errors
to become illuminated

I tell you there are rooftops
on which the moon stops

being a cold jewel
and one by one

the mountains begin their descent
from the chambers of a lost book

from *Verse*

CONTRIBUTORS' NOTES AND COMMENTS

RAE ARMANTROUT was born in Vallejo, California, in 1947. She teaches writing at the University of California, San Diego. She has published seven books of poetry and a memoir called *True* (Atelos, 1998). Her most recent books of poetry are *Made to Seem* (Sun and Moon Press, 1995), *The Pretext* (Green Integer, 2001), and *Veil: New and Selected Poems* (Wesleyan University Press, 2001). Her work was included in the 1988 and 2001 editions of *The Best American Poetry*.

Armantrout writes: " 'Up to Speed' is the title poem of the manuscript I'm working on. I think the poem, and much of the rest of the manuscript, is about the experience of time—the ways in which we try and fail to grasp it. The Sphinx's question to Oedipus ('What walks on four legs in the morning, on two at noon, on three at dusk?') is really about the nature of time. His clever answer ('man') leads him, well, you know where."

JOHN ASHBERY was born in Rochester, New York, in 1927. He is the author of more than twenty books of poetry, including *Some Trees,* which was selected by W. H. Auden for the Yale Younger Poets Prize of 1956, and *Self-Portrait in a Convex Mirror,* which won the poetry equivalent of the triple crown (the Pulitzer Prize, the National Book Award, and the National Book Critics Circle Award) in 1976. Ashbery is the Charles P. Stevenson, Jr., Professor of Language and Literature at Bard College. A Harvard alumnus, he gave that university's Norton lectures on Thomas Lovell Beddoes, John Clare, Laura Riding, Raymond Roussel, David Schubert, and John Wheelwright. The lectures were published under the title *Other Traditions* (Harvard University Press, 2000). *As Umbrellas Follow Rain* (Qua Books), *100 Multiple-Choice Questions* (Adventures in Poetry), and a reprint of *The Vermont Notebook* (with drawings by Joe Brainard; Granary Books and Z Press) were all published last year. In 2001 he was named state poet of New York, and in 2002 he received the

Wallace Stevens Award from the Academy of American Poets. A volume of his selected literary criticism is in the works. He divides his time between Hudson, New York, and New York City. He was guest editor of the inaugural volume of *The Best American Poetry* in 1988.

AMIRI BARAKA was born Everett LeRoi Jones in Newark, New Jersey, in 1934. He attended Rutgers University for two years and received his B.A. from Howard University. He served in the Air Force from 1954 until 1957. After moving to the Lower East Side of Manhattan, he married Hettie Cohen and began coediting the avant-garde literary magazine *Yugen* with her. He also founded Totem Press, which published works by Allen Ginsberg and Jack Kerouac. *Preface to a Twenty-Volume Suicide Note,* his first volume of poetry, appeared in 1961. From 1961 to 1963 he was coeditor, with Diane di Prima, of *The Floating Bear,* a literary newsletter. His increasing hostility toward and mistrust of white society was reflected in two plays, *The Slave* and *The Toilet,* both written in 1962. Nineteen sixty-three saw the publication of *Blues People: Negro Music in White America,* which he wrote, and *The Moderns: An Anthology of New Writing in America,* which he edited and introduced. His reputation as a playwright was established with the production of *Dutchman* at the Cherry Lane Theatre in New York on March 24, 1964. The controversial play subsequently won an Obie Award (for "best off-Broadway play") and was made into a film. In 1965, following the assassination of Malcolm X, Jones repudiated his former life and ended his marriage. In 1967 he married the African-American poet Sylvia Robinson (now known as Amina Baraka). His play *Home on the Range* was performed as a benefit for the Black Panther Party in 1968. That same year he became a Muslim, changing his name to Imamu Amiri Baraka. ("Imamu" means "spiritual leader.") From 1968 to 1975, he was chairman of the Committee for a Unified Newark, a black united-front organization. His play *Slave Ship* was widely reviewed. He was one of the chief organizers of the National Black Political Convention, which convened in Gary, Indiana, in 1972. In 1974 Baraka adopted a Marxist-Leninist philosophy and dropped the spiritual title "Imamu." He and Amina Baraka edited *Confirmation: An Anthology of African-American Women* (1983), which won an American Book Award from the Before Columbus Foundation. *The Autobiography of LeRoi Jones* was published in 1984. Since 1985 he has been a professor of Africana Studies at the State University of New York at Stony Brook. He is codirector, with his wife, of Kimako's Blues People, a community arts space. Amiri and Amina Baraka live in Newark, New Jersey.

CHARLES BERNSTEIN was born in New York City in 1950. He is the author of more than twenty collections of poetry and essays. His most recent books include *With Strings* and *My Way: Speeches and Poems,* both from the University of Chicago Press, and *Republics of Reality: 1975–1995,* from Sun and Moon Press. Bernstein is the editor of *Close Listening: Poetry and the Performed Word* (Oxford University Press) and *99 Poets: 1999: An International Poetics Symposium* (Duke University Press / boundary 2). He is executive director of the Electronic Poetry Center (epc.buffalo.edu) and the director of the poetics program at the State University of New York at Buffalo.

Bernstein writes: " '12" is made up of twelve twelves, with one flaw in the ointment. A motto might be detoured from Mallarmé:

> Not the desert clarity of my lamp
> But the blanched consequence of my intransigence

Or possibly from my nine-year-old son Felix:

> Nothing to bite
> but my tongue."

ANSELM BERRIGAN was born in Chicago, Illinois, in 1972 and grew up in New York City, where he lives with the poet Karen Weiser, after seven years in Buffalo and San Francisco. He currently works as a "communications consultant" for Baruch College and teaches at Rutgers University. He has published three chapbooks: *On the Premises* (GAS Editions, 1995), *They Beat Me Over the Head with a Sack* (Edge, 1998), and, with his brother, Edmund Berrigan, *In the Dream Hole* (Man, 2001). His full-length collections are *Integrity & Dramatic Life* (Edge, 1999) and *Zero Star Hotel* (Edge, 2002). He recently coedited, with Edwin Torres, the first issue of PO-eP, a new electronic journal.

Of "Zero Star Hotel," Berrigan writes: "These are four pages from a thirty-five-page poem written in the summer and fall of 2000. The form comes out of trying to figure out a different way to write after my stepfather, the British poet Douglas Oliver, died in April 2000. I was looking for a form that could handle having a foot in the public world while tracking the all-over-the-place consciousness grief was inciting. The title comes from overhearing the concierge of a recently shut-down Paris hotel describe it as having 'zero stars.' My brother and I usually stayed at this hotel when visiting Doug and our mother, as it was cheap, next door, and a lot like the apartment we grew up in."

FRANK BIDART was born in 1939 in Bakersfield, California. He didn't escape until 1957, when he began to study at the University of California at Riverside. "Escape" is an exaggeration; childhood and youth take too long, perhaps everywhere. He began graduate work at Harvard in 1962, studying with Reuben Brower and Robert Lowell. His most recent book of poems, *Desire* (Farrar, Straus and Giroux, 1997), received the 1998 Bobbitt Prize for Poetry from the Library of Congress and the Theodore Roethke Memorial Poetry Prize. His first chapbook, *Music Like Dirt* (Sarabande Books, 2002), is a sequence of poems; the sequence mixes memory and desire with the theme of making.

Bidart (who surely wrote the above) adds: "Think of 'Injunction' as the injunction heard by an artist faced with the forever warring elements of the world that proceed from the forever unreconciled elements of our nature. It is not meant to stand alone, but to be part of the tapestry of *Music Like Dirt.*"

JENNY BOULLY was born in Korat, Thailand, in 1976, to a Thai mother and an American father. She grew up in San Antonio, Texas, and has studied at Hollins University and at the University of Notre Dame. *The Body* was published by Slope Editions in 2002. She lives in Castroville, Texas.

Boully writes: "When I began writing "The Body" (which was originally published as a lyric essay in *Seneca Review*), I had an obsession with fragmentation: I had just read Kafka's 'masterpiece novel-fragments' *The Trial* as well as Roland Barthes's *A Lover's Discourse*. It didn't help that I was rereading the pre-Socratic philosophers and pasting my favorite excerpts from poems, essays, stories, and so forth on my walls. Fragmentation, incompleteness, the manner in which a book and a life are put together: these became fascinating to me. I knew I was writing some sort of fragmentary subtext to some life or other and then fell in love with the idea that not only do our individual lives have subtexts, real or imagined, but that life itself is the subtext to something else. I decided that whatever the story was, I would, as life so often seems to do, write the footnotes first and then construct the story later."

T. ALAN BROUGHTON was born in Bryn Mawr, Pennsylvania, in June 1936. He attended Exeter Academy, Harvard University, and the Juilliard School of Music, and received degrees from Swarthmore College and the University of Washington. He continues to play piano, although no longer for performance. In 1966 he began teaching writing at the

University of Vermont. The author of four novels, a collection of short stories, and six books of poetry, he visits Rome as often as he can but "would never want to live anywhere but in Burlington, Vermont, and Keene Valley, New York."

Of "Ballad of the Comely Woman," Broughton writes: "The first poem I wrote was a ballad. I was fifteen, living in Rome for one year with my parents, and attending a small school for English-speaking students. We were studying the traditional ballads of Scotland and England, and our teacher asked each of us to write a ballad for class discussion. I am not sure why I chose to write about Tecumseh, but perhaps I thought he was at least as heroic a figure as Sir Patrick Spens. Many of the poems I have written in the fifty years since have been narratives, fragments of narratives, or poems spoken in the voices of people who wish to tell their stories.

"In 1962 I began teaching, and until I retired in 2001, I often taught an introductory course in the reading of poetry. Over the course of so many years, some poems would seem essential to me, then fade or drop out of my classroom, only to reappear years later. But the early modern ballads never failed me.

"I like to run almost every day. With my feet in motion, no one talking to me, sometimes my mind not even talking to itself, I seem to be able to leave all my obsessions behind and take in whatever presents itself—rabbits, a fox, someone walking a dog, groundhogs, once even a bewildered deer. One day I was running and the ballad form started repeating itself in my head, not with words but in rhythms and sounds that had not yet formed into distinct syllables. At some point, those sounds did gather into words and phrases. I cut my run short by two miles in order to write them down, fearing they were written in the vanishing ink of dreams. What happened was 'Ballad of the Comely Woman.' Unusual for me, the poem was little changed subsequently. I suspect it came from some chamber of my mind where the scribe had already been hard at work without letting me know until endorphins unlocked the door."

MICHAEL BURKARD was born in Rome, New York, on January 1, 1947. He teaches in the MFA Program at Syracuse University and in the summer program at the Fine Arts Work Center in Provincetown, Massachusetts. He has taught in the past at Sarah Lawrence College and the University of Louisville and has also worked as a psychiatric aide, an alcoholism and addictions counselor, and a proofreader for Bloomingdale's catalogs. He has been writing songs and making drawings for many years.

His drawings (in collaboration with Maryalice Johnston) were part of the C-Scape Mapping Project 2001 Group Exhibition. A recording, *radio journal*, by musician/composer Edward Ruchalski, includes Burkard's text and spoken word (available on the Seagull Label). His books currently in print are *The Fires They Kept* (Metro Book Co., 1986), *My Secret Boat* (W. W. Norton, 1990), *Entire Dilemma* (Sarabande Books, 1997), *Unsleeping* (Sarabande Books, 2001), and *Pennsylvania Collection Agency* (New Issues Press, 2001). The latter contains the poem "What I Threw into the Grave." He has received two fellowships from the National Endowment for the Arts, two grants in poetry from the New York Foundation for the Arts, and, in 1988, a Whiting Writer's Award.

Burkard writes: "A notebook indicates I wrote 'What I Threw into the Grave' in December 1985. My memory tells me I was simply looking for some angle or idea that was new for me—and that I thought (perhaps indirectly off something some other writer wrote) the idea of what would I throw into a grave, *my* grave (although I see I didn't use "my" in the title—too close?)—might suit me. Carl was a person I knew years back when I lived in Cambridge, Massachusetts, and Mona was partly real, partly imagined. I had house-sat for Bill and Susan Mariner, so their name worked in a double sense—I was writing the poem in Maryland, I was living there. The Mariners had lived aptly by the sea—the sea was almost/just out their back windows. I think the list got more particular to me as I went along, but still very associational. I admit to rewriting this list many times over a dozen years, but for silly reasons—embarrassed by what was in it, trying to make it sound better or more important. I rarely sent out the poem, and not a lot of people saw it. I regret to say I don't know if the quoted material is from a source or something I wrote myself, or something overheard. I am surprised I ended the poem as soon as I did. I reverted as I usually do to the original version. This first draft is handwritten, almost illegible at times. It looks to me like a drawing headed sideways, even though the poem heads down. In hindsight it is clear to me that I was going through a difficult transition in my life, and I had recently thrown much into a grave of sorts."

ANNE CARSON was born in Toronto, Canada, in 1950 and teaches ancient Greek for a living. Knopf published her translation of the fragments of Sappho, with commentary, in 2002. A professor of classics at McGill University in Montreal, she has also taught recently at the University of Michigan and at Berkeley. Her books include *Glass, Irony and God* and *Men in the Off Hours* (Knopf, 2000). Her most recent book is *The*

Beauty of the Husband (Knopf, 2001). She has received a Guggenheim Fellowship. Her work appears in *The Best of the Best American Poetry, 1988–1997,* edited by Harold Bloom, and in the 2001 edition of *The Best American Poetry.*

Of "Opposed Glimpse of Alice James, Garth James, Henry James, Robertson James and William James," Carson writes: "Who does not wonder what other people's Sundays are like? I fear the Jameses did not."

ELIZABETH BILLER CHAPMAN was born in Boston in 1943. She attended Smith College, studied at the Shakespeare Institute as a Marshall Scholar in Britain, and received a Ph.D. from Columbia in 1969. Formerly a teacher of Renaissance literature as well as a psychotherapist, she lives in Palo Alto, California. She has taught at the Foothill College Writer's Conference and is a member of the Squaw Valley Community of Writers. In 1995 her chapbook, *Creekwalker,* won the (m)Other Tongue Press international competition. Her first full-length collection, *First Orchard,* was published by Bellowing Ark Press in 1999.

Of "On the Screened Porch," Chapman writes: "It is perhaps unusual, and certainly a privilege, to be able to return to the house I grew up in—and where my mother lives still—and have a meal on the same porch where my family used to eat suppers in warm weather some fifty years ago."

TOM CLARK was born in Oak Park, Illinois, in 1941. He is the author of numerous volumes of poetry, including *Stones* (Harper & Row, 1969), *Air* (Harper & Row, 1970), *Neil Young* (Coach House, 1971), *At Malibu* (Kulchur, 1975), *When Things Get Tough on Easy Street* (Black Sparrow, 1978), *Paradise Resisted* (Black Sparrow, 1984), *Disordered Ideas* (Black Sparrow, 1987), *Fractured Karma* (Black Sparrow, 1990), *Sleepwalker's Fate* (Black Sparrow, 1992), *Like Real People* (Black Sparrow, 1995), *Empire of Skin* (Black Sparrow, 1997), *White Thought* (Hard Press/The Figures, 1997), and *Cold Spring: A Diary* (Skanky Possum, 2000). He has also written novels, including *The Exile of Céline* (Random House, 1987) and *The Spell: A Romance* (Black Sparrow, 2000), as well as literary biographies, including *Jack Kerouac* (Harcourt Brace Jovanovich, 1984), *Charles Olson: The Allegory of a Poet's Life* (W. W. Norton, 1991), *Robert Creeley: The Genius of the American Common Place* (New Directions, 1993), and *Edward Dorn: A World of Difference* (North Atlantic, 2002). Since 1987 Clark has been a member of the core faculty in poetics at New College of California.

Of "Lullaby for Cuckoo," Clark writes: "A mechanistic universe constructed out of a hopeful human toolbox and featuring a helpful cuckoolike deity who conveniently pops out of this great invented toy clock to inform us our meanings are arriving on time—this is the ultimate *donnée* that the poem appears, perhaps ungratefully or perhaps at last realistically, to reject ... but not without registering a certain pathos, since if anything could seem more pathetic (in the picture the poem proposes) than human wishes and vanities, would it not be the vehicles chosen to objectify them?"

PETER COOLEY was born in Detroit in 1940 and grew up there and in the suburbs of the city. He graduated from Shimer College, which he entered before finishing high school, the University of Chicago, and the Writers' Workshop at the University of Iowa, where he received his Ph.D. Married and the father of three children, he is a professor of English at Tulane University. From 1970 to 2000, he was poetry editor of *North American Review.* He has published six books, five of them from Carnegie Mellon, which next year will bring out his new volume, *A Place Made of Starlight,* in which "Corpus Delicti" will appear. He has lived in New Orleans since 1975.

Of "Corpus Delicti," Cooley writes: "The death in Detroit of my mother, sister, and father, all the family I came from, in the year of the millennium no doubt led to a renewed obsession with one of poetry's most esteemed subjects. Identifying each body for cremation, which the funeral home forced me to do as next of kin, made me dwell (as if I hadn't done so enough in earlier poems!) on those I loved and hated as objects of study. I was thrown back to what I realized when I wrote my first poem in fifth grade and which reading Flaubert in college confirmed: the writer is always an observer. The same month my father died, I become a grandfather for the first time; perhaps that is why my speaker is waking to an awareness of his life and death? I found that the poem—like many of my more explicit grief poems—comfortably emerged as a sonnet. The moment of waking I regard as one of life's almost sacramental ones, which we are allowed to reenact each day."

CLARK COOLIDGE was born in Providence, Rhode Island, in 1939. He is a poet and a drummer. His most recent books are *Now It's Jazz—Writing on Kerouac and the Sounds* (Living Batch Press, 1999), *Alien Tatters* (Atelos, 2000), *On the Nameways Volume Two* (The Figures, 2001), and *Far Out West* (Adventures in Poetry, 2001). He resides in Petaluma, California.

Coolidge writes: " 'Traced Red Dot' is from a series of poems written with eye, ear, and backbrain on the satellite movie channels. Face colors, landscape, and voices, the taken and mistaken, mix in the endless mind. *The Pick-up Artist* and *The Thin Red Line* were on during this one."

RUTH DANON was born in Chicago, Illinois, in 1949. At the age of five she moved to Binghamton, New York, where she lived with her mother (a psychiatrist) and grandmother in an apartment on the grounds of the Binghamton State Hospital. This is the setting for a memoir she is currently writing. She received a B.A. from Bard College and a Ph.D. from the University of Connecticut. At present she runs the creative and expository writing programs at NYU's Paul McGhee Division, where she is also director of the summer intensive creative writing workshops. Two of her books have been published: a volume of literary criticism, *Work in the English Novel* (Croom-Helm), and a book of poems, *Triangulation from a Known Point* (Blue Moon–North Star Line). She lives in New York City with her husband, the painter Gary Buckendorf.

Danon writes: "My poems seem often like a wonderful mystery and never more so than after they are written. 'Long after (Mallarmé),' is such a mystery. At the time I wrote it I was feeling the heaviness of the millennial turn, wondering what was in store for all of us, and was teaching Mallarmé for the first time, feeling excited and awed. The last lines came first. I scribbled them into a notebook numerous times as if I were trying to get acquainted with them. Then came the Alaskan Airline crash. A good friend lost family members in that crash and I felt her devastation keenly. That event triggered the poem. I wrote it quickly, struck by the compression of the lines and the compression of emotion, which opened up some rhythmic possibilities and freed me to use rhyme. I'm grateful to Hermine Meinhard for publishing the poem in *3rd Bed* and honored that Robert Creeley confirmed her faith in this piece."

DIANE DI PRIMA was born in Brooklyn in 1934 and lived in Manhattan for many years. A founder of the New York Poets Theater, she edited, with Amiri Baraka (LeRoi Jones), the literary newsletter *The Floating Bear* from 1961 to 1963. In 1965 she moved to upstate New York, where she participated in Timothy Leary's psychedelic community at Millbrook. For the past thirty-two years she has lived in northern California. She is now at work on a study of Shelley's poetic use of traditional Western magic. Her thirty-five books of poetry and prose include *Pieces of a Song* (City Light Books, 1990), an expanded edition of her epic poem *Loba* (Penguin, 1998), and *Recollections of My Life as a Woman: The New York Years*

(Viking Press, 2001), an autobiographical memoir. An enlarged edition of *Revolutionary Letters* (Last Gasp Press, 2002) and a book of uncollected poems from the 1980s and '90s, entitled *The Poetry Deal* (Tia Chucha Press), are both scheduled to appear in 2002.

Of "Midsummer," di Prima writes: "This poem is a part of a manuscript entitled *Alchemical Studies*. It is a brief 'take' on how the processes of alchemy imbue the natural world."

THEODORE ENSLIN was born in Chester, Pennsylvania, in 1925. He studied music composition with Nadia Boulanger from 1943 to 1945 and decided to write full-time soon after. Recent books include *Then and Now: Selected Poems 1943–1993* (National Poetry Foundation, 1999), *Re-Sounding: Selected Later Poems* (Talisman House, 1999), and *Nine* (Spuyten Duyvil, 2002).

Enslin writes: "My life has been spent as a writer, and except for a few short periods, I have never held any bona fide position or job. I have drawn upon my training as a musician in my attempt to create a poetry which is in some respects cognate. I have often said that I would take it as a great compliment if I was referred to as a composer who used words instead of notes.

" 'Moon Cornering' was one of a handful of poems that came very easily. It may have occurred from a sighting during the 'bright moon' period of several years ago."

ELAINE EQUI was born in Oak Park, Illinois, in 1953. She is the author of *Surface Tension, Decoy,* and, most recently, *Voice-Over,* which won the San Francisco State Poetry Award. A new collection, *Reset,* is forthcoming from Coffee House Press in 2003. She teaches at New York University and in the graduate program at City College, and lives in New York City.

Equi writes: "When I first wrote 'O Patriarchy,' I thought it wasn't finished. It sat in my notebook awhile. I almost decided to trash it. I would have, too, but when I reread it, something in its tone amused me. I guess I like its overly deferential and obsequious manner—the way it's almost a ditty. By insisting on its own slightness, it seems to magnify the power relations at stake. I meant it as a playful comment on gender, but the disappearing act it describes (i.e., the fact that because power is everywhere and nowhere, there's never anyone to complain to) is certainly applicable to all sorts of other situations."

CLAYTON ESHLEMAN was born in Indianapolis, Indiana, in 1935. Since 1986, he has been a professor in the English Department at Eastern Michigan University in Ypsilanti. Black Sparrow Press has brought out thirteen collections of his poetry, the most recent of which, *My Devotion* (2002), includes the poem published here. Wesleyan University Press recently published a collection of his essays, *Companion Spider,* with a foreword by Adrienne Rich. Eshleman is also the main American translator of César Vallejo (*Trilce,* published by Wesleyan, 2000), Aimé Césaire (*Notebook of a Return to the Native Land,* cotranslated with Annette Smith, Wesleyan, 2001), and Antonin Artaud (*Watchfiends & Rack Screams,* Exact Change, 1995). In the 1960s and '70s he edited twenty issues of *Caterpillar* magazine; from 1981 to 2000, he edited forty-six issues of *Sulfur.* Since 1974 he has been engaged in fieldwork and research on Ice Age cave art. He and his wife lead a small tour to the Upper Paleolithic caves of southwestern France every June. In 2002 Wesleyan brought out his *Juniper Fuse: Upper Paleolithic Imagination and the Construction of the Underworld.*

Of "Animals out of the Snow," Eshleman writes: "For years I have worked on getting the full content of certain dreams into poems. At times I have kept a tape recorder by the bed to speak the dream into as soon as I awaken. Milton Kessler told me years ago about the gruesome circumstances of John Logan's death in Buffalo and had for years planned to write an elegy for Logan (Kessler died this past year and I do not know if such a poem will be found in his archive). In our epoch many animals have gone extinct. The animal revenge in the poem is one of many possible psychic responses to this tragedy. Logan's abrupt incapacitated presence in the poem, while enigmatic, was part of the dream, so I included it. In the psyche, things 'rhyme' (or become reflecting metaphors) in ways that reveal the abyss right below consciousness."

NORMAN FINKELSTEIN was born in New York City in 1954. He has published a collection of poems, *Restless Messengers* (University of Georgia Press, 1992), and three books of literary criticism, most recently *Not One of Them in Place: Modern Poetry and Jewish American Identity* (SUNY Press, 2001). For a number of years, he has been writing an ongoing serial poem called *Track.* The first two volumes are *Track* (Spuyten Duyvil, 1999) and *Columns* (Spuyten Duyvil, 2002). He lives in Cincinnati, Ohio, where he is a professor of English at Xavier University.

Of "Drones and Chants," Finkelstein writes: "I became friends with Armand Schwerner (1927–1999) during the last years of his life. I read with him on a number of occasions, and corresponded with him while writing about his poetry in my book *Not One of Them in Place,* though he died before the book appeared. My original intention for 'Drones and Chants' was simply as a presentation piece for Armand; sadly, it became an elegy.

"The poem is related to my thinking about ethnopoetics, a movement in which Armand played a crucial role, and about the self-consciousness that, I believe, must accompany the fundamentally romantic attempt to connect with the archaic and the 'primitive.' Armand understood these ironies at their deepest level, and that is one reason why his poem *The Tablets* is such an important work. I hope my poem will serve as a signpost, pointing the reader to Armand's extraordinary literary accomplishments."

JEFFREY FRANKLIN was born in 1954 and grew up in Chattanooga, Tennessee. He now lives in Denver, Colorado, and teaches at the University of Colorado at Denver. His book, *Serious Play: The Cultural Form of the Nineteenth-Century Realist Novel* (1999), was published by the University of Pennsylvania Press. A group of his poems was the corecipient of the 2001 Robert H. Winner Memorial Award from the Poetry Society of America.

Of "To a Student Who Reads 'The Second Coming' as Sexual Autobiography," Franklin writes: "This poem was sparked by a conversation about Yeats's 'The Second Coming' that I had with a student when I was a graduate teaching assistant. I experienced a pulmonary implosion while trying to appear—successfully, I hope—to take that student's seriously tendered interpretation seriously. The idea of allowing the student's comment to grow into the argument of an essay and then making the poem the professor's commentary upon that essay incubated for six years. I drafted the poem in fall 1998. My workshop colleagues at the time—Debra Kang Dean, Julie Fay, and Lillian Robinson—suggested revisions. When I returned to it, I realized that this parody (and homage) would be most effective if modeled more strictly on the original. Once I decided to use Yeats's end-words (with a few key modifications) and to conform to his meter, the poem fell quickly into place. Relevant to the poem is the joke about the husband who asks his wife, 'How about a quickie?' She responds, 'As opposed to what?' "

BENJAMIN FRIEDLANDER was born in New Orleans in 1959. His most recent books of poetry are *A Knot Is Not a Tangle* (Krupskaya Press, 2000) and *Algebriac Melody* (Zasterle Press, 1998). A selection of his *One*

Hundred Etudes appeared as Backwoods Broadside no. 59 (2001). With Donald Allen he edited *The Collected Prose of Charles Olson* (University of California Press, 1997). He teaches at the University of Maine at Orono, home of the National Poetry Foundation, where he coedits the scholarly journal *Sagetrieb: Poetry and Poetics after Modernism.*

Friedlander writes: " 'Independence Day' is part of a long poem called *One Hundred Etudes,* a series of poetic exercises in homage to Louis Zukofsky. The individual sections run in continuous sequence (divided only by 'Etude' number), and all are parsed into three-word lines and three-line stanzas—a prosody inspired by Zukofsky's *A.'* Every section also bears a dedication or epigraph, and these indicate a variety of things: dialogue and debate, friendship and debt, shared history, shared poetics. If my poem has no other value, however, let it serve as a reading list: Paul Beatty's poetry is incredible. Readers unfamiliar with his work should find a copy of *Joker, Joker, Deuce* right away."

GENE FRUMKIN was born in New York City in 1928. Among his books of poetry are *Comma in the Ear* (Living Batch, 1990), *Saturn Is Mostly Weather: Selected and Uncollected Poems* (Cinco Puntos, 1992), *The Old Man Who Swam Away and Left Only His Wet Feet* (La Alameda, 1998), and a chapbook, *Falling into Meditation* (Instress, 1999). He is a professor emeritus of English at the University of New Mexico and lives in Albuquerque.

Frumkin writes: " 'Surreal Love Life' is from a book-length series of poems entitled *Freud by Other Means* (La Alameda Press, 2002). It places Freud, the rationalist of the unconscious, in a context of living / 'loving' in an aesthetic for which he had no use. The surrealists of the 1920s adapted his thought to their outlook on the chaotic reality of World War I, when language in its narrow, ideational forms betrayed its deep sources, passing through the hidden darkness of the mind without penetrating it. The objective of the poem is to locate Freud in his own dream work, the collages of his thought as he investigates the quandaries of daily life.

"The poem is not typical of the series, which tries to focus on Freud as a subject of the imagination rather than as an exegete of surrealism before the fact. It is not a biography nor a study of his cases. The effort is to portray him and Jung and psychoanalysis itself as an event in language's continuing history."

FORREST GANDER was born in the Mojave Desert in California in 1956. He is a professor of English literature and the director of graduate creative writing at Brown University. His most recent book of poems, *Torn Awake*, was published by New Directions in 2001. His translations, *No Shelter: Selected Poems of Pura Lopez Colome* (Graywolf Press) and (with Kent Johnson) *Immanent Visitor: Selected Poems of Jaime Saenz* (University of California Press), appeared in 2002. He lives in Providence, Rhode Island.

Gander writes: " 'Carried Across' from *trans latus*. The experience of finding, in another country, that the stranger is not the other but the self, the selves. To read emotional traces written within self and world—jealousy, fear, desperation, humor, little ecstasies—to read the symbols—graffiti, a painted hand, retablos, codices—and even the animal gestuary—birdsong, lizard stare, swallow flight, slinking pariah dogs—as signs that lead to contemplation and suggest connected experiences across cultural, linguistic, and temporal borders. Out of those recognitions, the summons to responsibility. Despite the impossibility of accurate translation of either language or feeling, the heightened attentiveness, the proximities and ethical implications revealed in the act of translation, in the recognition of one's own inescapable foreignness and humility at the thresholds of the word."

PETER GIZZI was born in Alma, Michigan, in 1959 and grew up in Pittsfield, Massachusetts. His poetry publications include *Artificial Heart* (Burning Deck, 1998) and *Periplum* (Avec, 1992). He has received grants from the Fund for Poetry (1993), the Rex Foundation (1994), the Howard Foundation (1998), and the Foundation for Contemporary Performance Arts (1999). In 1994 he received the Lavan Younger Poets Award from the Academy of American Poets. His editing projects have included the magazine *o·blek: a journal of language arts* (1987–93), the anthology the *Exact Change Yearbook* (Exact Change/Carcanet, 1995), and the critical edition *The House That Jack Built: The Collected Lectures of Jack Spicer* (Wesleyan, 1998). He is currently teaching in the MFA Program at the University of Massachusetts at Amherst.

Gizzi writes: " 'Beginning with a Phrase from Simone Weil' was begun in fall 1999 while I was in residence at the Centre International de Poésie, Marseille. Because I was in the land of *Amors* I wanted to respond to the troubadour tradition by writing a series of songs, which I entitled 'Fin Amor.' The title of the series derives from the name of Bernart de Ventadorn's practice of trobar: *fin'amors* (pure love). And in keeping with the troubadour tradition this series of poems is also always about poetry. I felt by dropping the apostrophe one could read it both ways: *fin,* as in pure or fine, and *fin,* as in end. Marseille is where Simone Weil wrote her famous 'Spiritual Autobiography' in May 1942, just before she left France for the last time. Wanting to undercut a sentimental response to the end of the millennium, I turned to Weil's thinking about absence and, by implication, presence. The fugue form, with its repetitions and recapitulations, lent itself to an undoing of endings and supplied a counterpoint to the nostalgia for times past."

LOUISE GLÜCK was born in New York City in 1943. She is the author of ten books of poetry, including, most recently, *The Seven Ages* (Ecco/HarperCollins, 2001). She has received the National Book Critics Circle Award (for *The Triumph of Achilles,* 1985), the Bobbitt Prize (for *Ararat,* 1990), and the Pulitzer Prize (for *The Wild Iris,* 1992). She has also published a collection of essays, *Proofs and Theories: Essays on Poetry* (Ecco, 1994). She teaches at Williams College and lives in Cambridge, Massachusetts. In 1999 she was elected a Chancellor of the Academy of American Poets. She was guest editor of *The Best American Poetry 1993.*

ALBERT GOLDBARTH was born in Chicago in 1948 and currently lives in Wichita ("The Gateway to Boredom"), Kansas. He is Distinguished Professor of Humanities at Wichita State University. His books of poems include *Heaven and Earth: A Cosmology* (University of Georgia Press, 1992) and *Saving Lives* (Ohio State University Press, 2001). Both received the National Book Critics Circle Award in poetry. The most recent of his four collections of essays is *Many Circles: New and Collected Essays* (Graywolf Press, 2001). "Happily, my fingers have never touched a computer keyboard, and they intend to remain virginal in that way."

Of "The Gold Star," Goldbarth writes: "My feeling on 'commentary' is the same as it has been for earlier volumes in this series: my poems are intended to be self-sufficient and, I hope, more interesting and durable than any prose commentary I can addend to them—so why bother? I'm always amazed so many of my fellow poets feel otherwise, but it's beginning to occur to me that *the* universe doesn't generally function according to the rules of the *Goldbarthian* universe."

DONALD HALL was born in New Haven, Connecticut, in 1928. He lives on a farm in New Hampshire and supports himself by freelance writing. His fourteenth book of poems, *The Painted Bed,* appeared from Houghton Mifflin in 2002. Besides poetry, he has written books on baseball, the sculptor Henry Moore, and the poet Marianne Moore; children's books, including *Ox-Cart Man* (1979), which won the Caldecott Medal; short stories; and plays. He has edited more than two dozen textbooks and anthologies, including *The Oxford Book of Children's Verse in America* (1990), *The Oxford Book of American Literary Anecdotes* (1981), *New Poets of England and America* (with Robert Pack and Louis Simpson, 1957), and *Contemporary American Poetry* (1962; revised 1972). He served as poetry editor of *The Paris Review* from 1953 to 1962. He was the guest editor of *The Best American Poetry 1989*.

Hall writes: "It's a commonplace: Most poems, which intend or appear to say one thing, contain within themselves a contradiction to the apparent statement. I began and worked over 'Affirmation' in a bad time, in 2001, and I feared that the poem kept to the double track of depression and anger. When a magazine printed it, I received letters that referred to the conclusion as an actual affirmation, or at least an acceptance, of the losses and defeats that make up the poem. I would like to think so, not because I require the positive, but because I want in any poem a complexity accurate to human feeling, to its inescapable internal contradiction.

"This poem ends *The Painted Bed*. As I write this note, months before its publication, I feel strangely alien to the forthcoming book. But I do not denigrate the expression of earlier misery merely because I am happy in 2002."

MICHAEL S. HARPER was born in Brooklyn, New York, in 1938. He is University Professor at Brown University, where he has taught since 1970, and he was named the first poet laureate of the state of Rhode Island. He has twice been nominated for the National Book Award. His most recent books of poetry are *Honorable Amendments* (1995) and *Songlines in Michaeltree* (1999), both from the University of Illinois Press. He is the coeditor of the anthologies *Every Shut Eye Ain't Asleep* (Little, Brown, 1994) and *The Vintage Anthology of African American Poetry* (2000).

Of "TCAT serenade: 4 4 98 (New Haven)," Harper writes: "I was invited to Yale for a dramatic presentation of Seamus Heaney's play, TCAT, or *The Cure at Troy,* and though I was asked to perform on a panel, I had already written my response in the form published in *Harvard Review*. I also wrote out a reading of the parable of Philoctetes as an interpretation of the racial situation in the Americas, particularly North America. Heaney, as a colonial, victimized by the aftermath of the British Empire, has his own kettle of fish re Northern Ireland; Edmund Wilson's take is another, but the date of Martin Luther King, Jr.'s, death day, April 4, sent me in another direction, that of 'intentional suffering' as a philosophical assumption, that nonviolence has a particular resonance for the spiritual contributions to philosophy as an active ingredient in 'lasting' through the wilderness of American racism. I had already written about the four Birmingham girls blown up in the 16th Street church in a poem called 'American History' and did not want to repeat myself. Poets find their voices when they articulate the wishes of the dead, particularly those slain as sacrificial talismans to a larger frame of existence. Hence the spirituals, the ritual of resurrection as practiced by the black church, and the great songs of redemption: 'every time I hear the spirit I will pray'; or 'I been down so long that down don't worry me'; or 'I don't know why my mother wants to stay here for, this old world ain't been no friend to her.' Heaney's worldview of canonical storytelling in a paradigmatic frame of the ancestors is ritual ground for any poet whose testifying is connected with extreme pressure and extreme sacrifice. The duty of the poet is to conjure that pressure where the victim, in ritual sacrifice, is given voice (intentional suffering)."

EVERETT HOAGLAND was born in Philadelphia in 1942, and he grew up in that city. He graduated from Lincoln University and from Brown University's graduate creative writing program. His poetry first got a national readership with Clarence Major's *The New Black Poetry* (1968) and Dudley Randall's *The Black Poets* (1970). His first collection of poetry with national distribution was *Black Velvet,* published by Broadside Press. His most recent books are *This City* (Spinner Publications, 1998) and . . . *Here.* . . , *New and Selected Poems* (Leapfrog Press, 2002). He teaches African-American literature and poetry writing workshops at the University of Massachusetts at Dartmouth in North Dartmouth, Massachusetts.

Of "you: should be shoo be," Hoagland writes: "This is a tribute/poem to/about the uniquely influential poet Everett LeRoi Jones / Amiri Baraka. It speaks to the defiant spirit that has threaded the overlapping periods of his intellectual development as an activist artist from the late 1950s through his participation (and mine) at the National Poetry Foundation's conference on the University of Maine's Orono campus during early summer in 2000. I read part of the first draft to Amiri and Amina Baraka during a private off-campus lunch with them during that conference, and I was pleased by Baraka's laughter where my poem says his early 1960s existential/beat/bohemian poetry was 'too hip for words.'

"Influential? For four decades his work has modeled not only what like-minded practitioners should write about but how it can be written. And what other American poet directly inspired a large number of people to actually reenvision themselves, redefine themselves, rename themselves, and name their children the way Baraka's poetry and prose did re: the young, Afrocentric African Americans of my generation during the second half of the 1960s?

"If Baraka had written only *Dutchman,* he would be a significant twentieth-century literary figure. But he has prolifically written so much more that is beautifully true, relevant—indeed, revolutionary. And what other contemporary poet has made a more admirable, expert prose contribution to American music, musicology, and social/cultural criticism?

"And since he rejected cultural chauvinism for a Marxist-Leninist worldview three decades ago, consistent with his beliefs he has remained accessible both in word and in person. No American poet in my lifetime has more actively pursued his or her truths than Amiri Baraka. Indeed, his politics/ethics/poetic are all one. Baraka acts in the afterlife of his words. No living poet more truly keeps his or her word(s)."

FANNY HOWE was born in Buffalo, New York, in 1940. She studied at Stanford University, graduating in 1962, and has lived mostly in New England and California. Her novels include *The Lives of a Spirit, The Deep North, Saving History,* and *Nod* (all from Sun and Moon Press) and *Indivisible* from Semiotexte/MIT Press. Some of her poetry (appearing from small presses for many years) was recently published as *Selected Poems* by the University of California Press (2000), and was awarded the 2001 Lenore Marshall Poetry Prize from the Academy of American Poets and *The Nation* magazine. A collection of short stories, called *Economics,* is due out in 2002 from Flood Editions. She is a professor of literature at the University of California at San Diego.

Of "9-11-01," Howe writes: "This poem was drawn from notes and an earlier poem written during the Gulf War, when I lived in San Diego, and watched the military planes flying out from Miramar Air Force Base to the Pacific. The sense of there being no difference between one desert and another, given the magnitude of attacks by air, was revived by the events of September 11, 2001, as was the end game of strict materialism."

RONALD JOHNSON was born in Ashland, Kansas, in 1935. He attended the University of Kansas, joined the army, and eventually received his bachelor's degree from Columbia. He moved to New York City as a young man. For three years he walked the Appalachian Trail and the English countryside with the poet Jonathan Williams. In 1969 he settled in San Francisco, where he lived until the early 1990s. He died in Topeka, Kansas, in March 1998. Some of his books are *A Line of Poetry, a Row of Trees* (Jargon, 1964), *Book of the Green Man* (W. W. Norton, 1967), *Valley of the Many-Colored Grasses* (W. W. Norton, 1969), *Songs of the Earth* (Grabhorn-Hoyem, 1970), *RADIOS* (Sand Dollar, 1977), *ARK: The Foundations* (North Point, 1980), *ARK 50* (E. P. Dutton, 1984), *ARK* [complete] (Living Batch, 1996), *To Do as Adam Did: Selected Poems* (Talisman House, 2000), and *The Shrubberies* (Flood Editions, 2001). He is also the author of several cookbooks, most notably *The American Table*, considered a masterpiece of American regional cooking, and recently reissued by Silver Spring Books. Robert Creeley has called Johnson "one of the defining peers of my own imagined company of poets."

Peter O'Leary, who edited Johnson's posthumous volume, *The Shrubberies,* which includes the poem in this book, writes: "The manuscript was left incomplete at his death. He left no formal sense of an organizing structure. His instructions to me were to 'prune' the 'Shrubs.' RJ wrote on the typewriter, so all of the poems in this manuscript are typed out, as are any corrections. When he was satisfied with a version of a poem he had been revising, he would draw a box around it in ballpoint pen. All of the poems in this selection are complete poems."

MAXINE KUMIN was born in Philadelphia in 1925. She was educated at Radcliffe College. With her husband she migrated in the 1970s to an old farm in New Hampshire, where they have raised horses and vegetables. Her twelfth book of poems, *The Long Marriage,* was published by W. W. Norton in 2001. She was the nation's Poet Laureate in 1980–81, when the position was known as Consultant in Poetry. She received the Pulitzer Prize for *Up Country: Poems of New England* (1972). She has written a memoir, *Inside the Halo and Beyond: The Anatomy of a Recovery* (W. W. Norton, 2000); four novels; a collection of short stories; more than twenty children's books; and four books of essays, most recently *Always Beginning: Essays on a Life in Poetry* (Copper Canyon, 2000) and *Women, Animals, and Vegetables* (W. W. Norton, 1994).

Kumin writes: " 'Flying' came to me episodically; it wasn't, alas, sent by the Muse, but stuttered its way into being little by little and underwent lots of revisions. I think it is a by-product of my advancing years. The distant past has acquired an unreliable sheen of glamour and I find myself dipping into early memories and hearsays with enthusiasm."

BILL KUSHNER was born in New York in 1931 and now works at nothing except poetry and playwriting. A 1999 recipient of a New York Foundation for the Arts poetry fellowship, he has had five books of poems published, most recently *He Dreams of Waters* (Rattapallax Press, 2000) and *That April* (United Artists Books, 2000). All of his books can be obtained from Small Press Distribution.

JOSEPH LEASE was born in Chicago in 1960 and was educated at Columbia, Brown (MFA, 1993), and Harvard (Ph.D., 1997). He is the author of a book of poems, *Human Rights* (Zoland Books), and a chapbook, *My Sister Life* (Jensen/Daniels). Thomas Fink's book *A Different Sense of Power: Problems of Community in Late Twentieth-Century U.S. Poetry* (Associated University Presses, 2001) includes extensive close readings of Lease's longer poems. Lease teaches at at Central Michigan University. Robert Creeley chose a sampler of seven of his poems for *Boston Review*.

Of " 'Broken World' (For James Assatly)," Lease writes: "When I met James Assatly in 1991, he was completing his novel *Hejira*. By the spring of 1992, when he graduated from Brown with his MFA, James had grown increasingly ill and was living at home with his parents. In 1993 he died in Boston of an AIDS-related illness. In an interview Edmund White, with whom James worked closely at Brown, called *Hejira* a 'remarkable novel . . . As long as *we* live, *we'll* remember that book.' I wrote this poem to honor James and his book, and to mourn all the words and worlds that were lost when we lost him. He was one of the smartest, toughest, most gifted people I knew then or have known since. He died on the morning of his thirty-first birthday—March 25, 1993. His novel remains unpublished."

TIMOTHY LIU was born in San Jose, California, in 1965. His first book of poems, *Vox Angelica* (Alice James Books, 1992), received the Norma Farber First Book Award from the Poetry Society of America. His other books are *Burnt Offerings* (Copper Canyon, 1995), *Say Goodnight* (Copper Canyon, 1998), and *Hard Evidence* (Talisman, 2001). He is the editor of *Word of Mouth: An Anthology of Gay American Poetry* (Talisman, 2000). He is on the faculty of William Paterson University and has held teaching appointments as the 2001 Distinguished Visiting Writer at the University of North Carolina at Wilmington and at the University of Michigan. He lives in Hoboken, New Jersey.

Of "Felix Culpa," Liu writes: "Our agon has ever been transgression. We are dragged through the mud as the paradises of our past recede. We hunt for diamonds knowing all is glittering paste. The facets are cut and polished nonetheless until we see our many selves reflected back. Reduced. Our animal nature not mirrored but imprisoned by laws we did not create. The lyric as prism to a world of undivided light that was never ours. To eschew 'original sin' in favor of a 'fortunate fall'! But who among us is equal to Milton in all his grandiloquent pomp? Surely poesy is on its last leg, slouching toward a *Götterdämmerung* that awaits us all."

NATHANIEL MACKEY was born in Miami, Florida, in 1947. He is the author of three books of poetry: *Eroding Witness* (University of Illinois Press, 1985), *School of Udhra* (City Lights Books, 1993), and *Whatsaid Serif* (City Lights Books, 1998). *Strick: Song of the Andoumboulou 16–25,* a compact disc recording of poems read with musical accompaniment (Royal Hartigan, percussion; Hafez Modirzadeh, reeds and flutes), was released in 1995 by Spoken Engine Company. Three volumes of his continuing prose composition, *From a Broken Bottle Traces of Perfume Still Emanate,* have thus far appeared: *Bedouin Hornbook* (Callaloo Fiction Series, 1986; second edition: Sun and Moon Press, 1997), *Djbot Baghostus's Run* (Sun and Moon Press, 1993), and *Atet A.D.* (City Lights Books, 2001). He is the editor of the literary magazine *Hambone* and coeditor (with Art Lange) of the anthology *Moment's Notice: Jazz in Poetry and Prose* (Coffee House Press, 1993). He teaches literature at the University of California at Santa Cruz.

JACKSON MAC LOW was born in Chicago in 1922. Educated at the University of Chicago and Brooklyn College, he has written poems, music, performance pieces, essays, plays, and radio works, and is a multimedia performance artist, usually with his wife, Anne Tardos. His publications since 1985 include *Representative Works: 1938–1985* (Roof Books, 1986), *Pieces o' Six: Thirty-three Poems in Prose* (Sun and Moon Press, 1992), *42 Merzgedichte in Memoriam Kurt Schwitters* (Station Hill, 1994), *Barnesbook* (Sun and Moon Press, 1996), *20 Forties* (Zasterle, 1999), and the CD *Open Secrets,* with Anne Tardos and seven instrumentalists (Experimental Intermedia, 1993). Granary Books in New York will soon publish a book of his performance scores (1955 to present). He received the Wallace Stevens Award from the Academy of American Poets. He lives in New York City.

Of "And Even You Elephants? (Stein 139/Titles 35)," Mac Low writes: "Having written poetry since 1937 in many ways, unusual, well-known, and traditional, I devised and often utilized chance-operational methods in the years 1954 to 1960. I was inspired by John Cage's music of the early 1950s and his Zen Buddhist rationale for his chance-operational methods, though my methods differed from his. Then, in 1960, I devised 'acrostic reading-through text selection,' whereby one reads a text and finds successively words or larger verbal units beginning with the letters of a 'seed text' (often the source's title). In 1963 I devised 'diastic reading-through text selection,' whereby one finds words or larger units that have the letters of a seed text in positions corresponding to those they occupy in the seed text's words. I wrote many poems by this method. Mistakenly, I thought reading-through methods were chance operational until about 1990, when I realized that they were rather 'deterministic' (a term suggested by my son, Mordecai-Mark): their outputs, when one uses the same source and seed texts, are always the same. Those of chance operations always differ. After writing nonmethodically 1989–98, I returned to diastic text selection (using Professor Charles O. Hartman's digital automation) in 1998–2000, using texts or passages by Gertrude Stein as source and seed texts, to write 161 poems. ('Titles' is a subset of the series 'Stein,' for which the seed texts are titles of works by Stein.) I usually did not accept the raw outputs of the diastic method, but revised them into normative sentences, retaining the root morphemes of nouns, verbs, adjectives, and adverbs but allowing changes of affixes, word order, and 'helping words.' The output of the method became material for poetic composition. Rather than accepting contingency, I engaged with it—and still do."

STEVE MALMUDE was born in Manhattan in 1940. After twelve years working as a carpenter for the New York City Housing Authority, he recently retired to Maine. His four books of poems are *Catting* (Adventures in Poetry, 1972), *From Roses to Coal* (Shell Press, 1980), *I Got to Know* (Goodbye Books, 1997), and *The Bundle* (Subpress/Goodbye Books, 2002).

Malmude writes: "'Perfect Front Door' is about my job and the news, which go together because I listen to the radio as I work. It's one of many poems in a form I've used for years: four rhymed quatrains. I like them simple, resonant, like chimes or jokes, and moving."

SARAH MANGUSO was born in 1974, grew up in Wellesley, Massachusetts, and was educated at Harvard University and the University of Iowa. She is the author of *The Captain Lands in Paradise* (Alice James Books, 2002).

This is her second appearance in the *Best American Poetry* series. She lives in Brooklyn and makes a living by editing newspaper copy.

Of "Address to Winnie in Paris," Manguso writes: "This was my first (and, so far, only) commissioned poem. As payment, Harris took me out to dinner. Winnie is now engaged to a man named Tom."

HARRY MATHEWS was born in New York City in 1930. His most recent books are *The Way Home: Selected Longer Prose* (Atlas Press, London, 1999) and *Sainte Catherine,* a novella written in French (Éditions P.O.L, Paris, 2000). He is a member of the OuLiPo, the French organization of writers and mathematicians committed to the invention and application of constrictive poetic forms. At present he divides his time between France and Key West, Florida.

Mathews writes: "My intention in composing 'Butter & Eggs' was to create poetry unlike any I had previously written. It would be instructive, devoted to everyday subject matter, and eschew not only Oulipian but traditional poetic resources such as metaphor; the result all the same had to be unmistakably poetry. But what is unmistakably poetic? Readers know; but of course they may not agree."

DUNCAN MCNAUGHTON was born in Boston, Massachusetts, in 1942. He has lived in California since the early 1970s and now lives in San Francisco. He has also spent time in Syria and Cyprus. He has taught classics, Oriental studies, and American and British literature. He has written more than a dozen books, including *another set / of circumstance* (Hawkhaven Press, 1998), *the wrapped church* (Blue Millennium Press/AIOU, 1996), *Kicking the Feather* (First Intensity Press, 1996), *Valparaiso* (Listening Chamber, 1995), and *The Pilot* (Blue Millennium Press, 1991). He recently translated, from the Italian, Dario Villa's *Venus Strapazzata dai Lunatici (Venus Ill-Treated by the Odd Ones)* (Blue Millennium Press, 2001).

McNaughton writes: "Insofar as one may explain any of this, conscious grounds of my work are myth, cosmology, secular mind; historical geography; and the inexhaustibly heartening lore of the poem across space and time, not only what it betrays one into but as well how indifferently it does so.

" 'Quarry' in both senses: object of the hunt; subterranean site of harvest of particular stone. Having been occupied in Phoenician studies for a while, was a few years ago detoured to Crete by way of photo sent me by Peter Downsbrough, underground *carrière* in south of France, while reading Durrell's *Cefalu/The Dark Labyrinth;* Cypriot/Paphian investigations plunked into late 'Minoan' stuff. Turns out to be aspect of work thirty years ago in Shakespeare's *Sonnets:* reality of 'labyrinth'; its own terms of manifestation of itself and its persons; its want of simple location. That is, who are the persons, really; where do they come from and what are their contexts; to what realities do their presences attest? These are thirteen of nineteen steps of the work, no explanation for that count, nor for the other stipulation it declared, that the word 'and' appear only in substantive function. One doesn't get to choose who or what one falls in love with, nor to presume why or what's next. In a more recent piece apparently ancillary to 'The Quarry' friend minotaur spoke in amusingly sane likeness of Philip Whalen."

W. S. MERWIN was born in New York City in 1927 and has also lived in Spain, England, France, Mexico, and Hawaii. His most recent books include *The Pupil* (2001), a translation of Dante's *Purgatorio* (2000), and *The River Sound* (1999), all from Knopf. *Flower & Hand* (1997) and *East Window* (1999), his translations of Asian poetry, have appeared from Copper Canyon Press. He has received the Pulitzer Prize (for *The Carrier of Ladders*), the PEN Translation Prize, the Dorothea Tanning Prize from the Academy of American Poets, and an award from the Lila Wallace–Reader's Digest Fund.

Of "To My Father's Houses," Merwin writes: "My father was a Presbyterian minister who came from rural western Pennsylvania. His first churches, and his last, were country churches or small-town ones, with small old manses like old farmhouses. He seemed always to covet one of his own, a kind of half-secret attraction, never quite practical, never part of the rest of his life."

PHILIP METRES was born in San Diego, California, on July 4, 1970, and grew up in the suburbs of Chicago. He received his Ph.D. and MFA from Indiana University in 2001. He teaches at John Carroll University in Cleveland, where he lives with his wife, Amy Breau, to whom "Ashberries: Letters" is dedicated. His poems and translations of Russian poets have appeared in the anthologies *In the Grip of Strange Thoughts: Russian Poetry in a New Era* (Zephyr, 1999) and *Dialogue Through Poetry* (2001). His translation, *A Kindred Orphanhood: Selected Poems of Sergey Gandlevsky,* is forthcoming. He has received a fellowship from the National Endowment of the Arts. When he reads his biography written this way, he does not recognize himself.

Of "Ashberries: Letters," Metres writes: "'There is a word for 'outside.' When you say 'outside,' you say 'on the street,' even where there is no street outside, just a dirt path. Down the street that was a street, past the train station, the School of Forest Technology allowed me to scrimmage with their hoops squad. After practice, the boys would pull out Marlboros and hang out in locker-room haze. Once a cow wandered through the center of campus. Getting lost requires a sense of place in the first place. I went to Moscow (on a Thomas J. Watson Fellowship in 1992–93) because poetry was said to 'matter' there. When I said this, my hosts chuckled: poetry is okay but it can't buy sausage. Once a kid offered to sketch my picture for '500 rubbles.' One poet told me that, almost overnight, her life savings of rubles couldn't buy a sausage. The first word I did not know was 'arbuz.' A big apple, they explained. Straight from the airport, we stopped off the highway, where a line of trucks spilled open with the big apples. We spent the rest of the ride spitting watermelon seeds."

MỘNG-LAN was born in Saigon, Vietnam, in 1970 and came with her family to the United States at the age of five. Although her three brothers and one sister followed their parents by becoming medical doctors in the United States, she took up painting and was awarded several art scholarships while in high school in Houston. In her senior year one of her paintings was selected for exhibition in the Capitol Building in Washington, DC. Her paintings have been exhibited in the Museum of Fine Arts in Houston and galleries in the San Francisco Bay Area. In her early twenties, she turned increasingly to writing, particularly poetry. She took her MFA at the University of Arizona, where she also taught writing and literature, and then won a two-year Stegner Fellowship at Stanford University. Her book *Song of the Cicadas* received the Juniper Prize and was published by the University of Massachusetts in 2001. She has a passion for Latin dance, particularly salsa and Argentine tango.

Mộng-Lan writes: " 'Trail,' from my second book, *Daguerreotypes of Sleep*, is an experiment with form—the form of the poem corresponding to the form of one's emotions, in particular the emotional extremes experienced in times of crisis. The poem finds itself exploring divinity in nature as well as in ourselves, and the signs of divinity manifest in nature. The speaker of the poem is on an arduous journey. Through sometimes fragmented language, sometimes hypnotic trancelike run-on sentences, the speaker is exploring the nature of relationships with the self and the beloved in our disjointed world."

JENNIFER MOXLEY was born in 1964 and grew up in San Diego, California. As an adult she has lived in Seattle, San Francisco, Providence, and Paris. At present she lives in Orono, Maine, where she works as a typesetter for the National Poetry Foundation and a lecturer at the University of Maine. She has been the poetry editor for *The Baffler* magazine since 1997. Her books of poems include *Imagination Verses* (Tender Buttons, 1996) and *The Sense Record* (Edge, 2002).

Of "Behind the Orbits," Moxley writes: "In addition to being the path of a celestial body, an 'orbit' is an eye socket. Therefore this poem might be said to occur entirely *behind* the eyes, as the opening lines indicate. It was written a month or so after I'd moved to Maine, in the wake of a rather fervent reading of E. A. Robinson's *Collected Poems*. I was, as my mom used to say, 'bowled over' by this famous Mainer's trenchant insights into the American psyche as well as by his skillful handling of the metrical line. Though I knew I could never approach his talent for writing blank verse, I thought I'd give it a sportsman's try. The result was 'Behind the Orbits.' But what is this poem about? Well, I'd say it is about the regret that builds up as a result of failing to be present for the most crucial moments in our lives, in this case, the death of a loved one."

EILEEN MYLES was born in Cambridge, Massachusetts, in 1949. She is a freelance poet, journalist, and teacher living in New York. ("In general, I travel, read, and write.") Her books include *Skies* (Black Sparrow, 2001), *on my way* (Faux Press, 2001), *Cool for You* (Soft Skull, 2000), *School of Fish* (Black Sparrow, 1997), *Chelsea Girls* (Black Sparrow, 1994), *Maxfield Parrish* (Black Sparrow, 1995), and *Not Me* (Semiotext(e), 1991). She recently taught at Pratt Institute in Brooklyn.

Of "Sympathy," Myles writes: "I experience writing poems as the chance to make a little movie. This one moves from autobiography (voice-over) to landscapey-ness, being linguistic, bait and switch (the woman I imagined flirting with me was nuts) and finally praying to god and sex, as usual. Not just for me but for everyone. I would like to replace the poet with the whole human race and am attempting that again here, in 'Sympathy.' "

MAGGIE NELSON was born in San Francisco in 1973. She is the author of *Not Sisters* (with Cynthia Nelson) (Soft Skull Press, 1996) and *The Scratch-Scratch Diaries,* featured in *AGNI* / Graywolf Press's *Take Three: 3 AGNI New Poets Series* (1998). Her first full-length book, *Shiner,* was published by Hanging Loose Press in 2001. In addition to writing a dissertation at the City University of New York about women of the so-called New York School, she has been working on an experimental narrative about the life and death of her aunt Jane, who was murdered in 1969. She currently teaches poetry at Wesleyan University and lives in Brooklyn, where she serves as a coeditor of the literary magazine *Fort Necessity*.

Of "Sunday Night," Nelson writes: "Whenever I title a poem '——— Night,' there's a good chance it has something to do with feeling like a shut-in, even if only for one night. In this poem I think I'm trying to talk myself into finding the right imaginative space to write from, or just to inhabit; whether that space be meditative or erotic or intellectual or vacuous or some combination thereof, the real problem is (as always) how to make yourself at home in your own mind. At the center of the poem lies the statement 'Powder is what's left/after the ideas have died,' which is a play on the remark that poetry begins when ideas (qua ideas) have died. I think that's from John Cage, but I'm not sure (I have been trying to remember the line's literal source, and will probably think of it the moment this goes into print). But it might as well have come from Cage, as it's related to his famous comments in *Lecture on Nothing:* 'I have nothing to say / and I am saying it. . . . Our poetry now / is the realization that we possess nothing.' Those twin notions have been very important and liberating to me, so it shouldn't come as any surprise that I don't feel as though many of the lines in 'Sunday Night' belong to me: the bit about the malt-vs.-milkshake is something I was instructed to tell customers when I worked at a dessert counter; my stepfather told me the story of the truck 'the size of Wisconsin' that dumped compost in his yard; the last line is one of my favorite messages from a fortune cookie. It occurs to me that there might be a greater point here—something about how our words and experiences are inextricable from those of others, and that this may be so even in (or especially in) one's lonelier moments—but I think I'll leave off there."

CHARLES NORTH was born in New York City in 1941. An active musician in his youth, he played clarinet with his first orchestra at the age of thirteen and spent summers at the music program in Interlochen, Michigan. He did his undergraduate work at Tufts and graduate studies at Columbia. The recipient of two fellowships from the National Endowment for the Arts and several Fund for Poetry Awards, he has published eight collections of poetry, most recently *New and Selected Poems* (Sun and Moon Press, 1999) and *The Nearness of the Way You Look Tonight* (Adventures in Poetry, 2000), which was a finalist for the inaugural Phi Beta Kappa Poetry Award. His poem "Shooting for Line" was included in *The Best American Poetry 1995*. With James Schuyler he edited *Broadway: A Poets and Painters Anthology* (Swollen Magpie, 1979) and *Broadway 2* (Hanging Loose, 1989). In 1998 Hanging Loose published his *No Other Way: Selected Prose*. He has written art criticism for *Art in America*, has worked in publishing, and is poet-in-residence at Pace University.

ALICE NOTLEY was born in Bisbee, Arizona, in 1945 and grew up in Needles, California. Her most recent books are *Disobedience* (2001) and *Mysteries of Small Houses* (1998), both from Penguin. She received an award in literature from the American Academy of Arts and Letters, as well as the Poetry Society of America's Shelley Award in 2001. She lives in Paris, France.

Of "Haunt," Notley writes: "The chantlike part at the end of the poem was suggested by a ceremony performed by Ecuadorian sorcerers, as described in *Les Appeleurs d'âmes* by Sabine Hargous. Otherwise the poem is simply one of grief."

D. NURKSE was born in New York City in 1949. His seven books of poetry include *The Fall* (Knopf, 2002), *The Rules of Paradise* (Four Way Books, 2001), *Leaving Xaia* (Four Way Books, 2000), and *Voices over Water* (Graywolf, 1993/Four Way Books, 1996). He has received two National Endowment for the Arts fellowships, two grants from the New York Foundation for the Arts, and the Whiting Writers' Award. He lives in Brooklyn.

Nurkse writes: "I've always wondered why Tolstoy's remark 'Happy families are all alike; every unhappy family is unhappy in its own way' became a cliché so easily. In 'Snapshot from Niagara' happiness is a scary, unpredictable force, which the poem doesn't understand, and only recognizes at the last minute. This poem, like so many others, is also about the life we don't live. I planned several trips to the falls. Something always defeated me—the sheer size of the region, the illusion that I knew what I would find."

SHARON OLDS was born in San Francisco, California, in 1942. Educated at Stanford and Columbia universities, she won the San Francisco Poetry Center Award for her first collection, *Satan Says* (University of Pittsburgh Press, 1980) and the National Book Critics Circle Award for her second, *The Dead & the Living* (Knopf, 1983). Her other books of poetry are *Blood, Tin, Straw* (1999), *The Gold Cell* (1997), *The Wellspring* (1995), and *The Father* (1992), all from Knopf. Named New York State Poet in 1998, Olds teaches in the graduate program in creative writing at New York University. Her next collection of poems, *The Unswept Room*, is forthcoming from Knopf. She lives in New York City.

Of "Frontis Nulla Fides," Olds writes: "The end is said by Duncan to Malcolm about Cawdor (*Macbeth*, act I, scene iv); the title is from Juvenal (*Satires*)."

GEORGE OPPEN was born in New Rochelle, New York, on April 24, 1908. As a young man in New York City, he fell into company with Louis Zukofsky and Charles Reznikoff, who took up the example of William Carlos Williams, intent on reclaiming Pound's Imagism from the influence of Amy Lowell and other "Amygists." Out of this nexus of like-minded poets the Objectivist Movement was born. In 1935 Oppen turned his back on his life as an artist and for the next five years worked as a strike organizer, first in Brooklyn and later in Utica, New York, for the Communist Party. In 1942 he was drafted into the United States Army. Shortly before V-E day, he suffered multiple wounds from an exploding shell. After the war, George and Mary Oppen settled in Huntington Beach, California, where the poet employed himself first as a housing contractor, then as a maker of hi-fi cabinets. In 1962 he published *The Materials,* his second collection of verse. It was followed three years later by *This Is Which* (New Directions, 1965). In 1968 his third collection of verse, *Of Being Numerous* (New Directions), was awarded the Pulitzer Prize. *Seascape: Needle's Eye* (Samac Press) was published in 1972, and his last collection, *Primitive* (Black Sparrow Press), edited by Mary Oppen, appeared in 1978. He died on July 7, 1984, in Sunnyside, California, a victim of Alzheimer's disease. His *New Collected Poems* was published by New Directions in 2002 and includes *Of Being Numerous.*

Stephen Cope, who edited "Twenty-six Fragments," explains that "The Last Words of George Oppen" was "the name given by archivists (in collaboration with Mary Oppen) to twenty-six fragments of writing—scrawled on envelopes and other small pieces of paper—posted to the walls of George Oppen's study and gathered after his death. Some of these fragments were numbered by Oppen, others were not. One fragment (#12) was found written in pencil on Oppen's wall. Although these are among the last writings Oppen is known to have produced, there is no way of determining their exact date of composition, nor does their content suggest any conscious desire on Oppen's part to mark them as either conclusive or final. Thus, I have adopted a less misleading title.

"#14 is a misquote from William Bronk's poem 'Virgin and Child with Music and Numbers.' Bronk's line reads: 'Still, the singing was and is.'"

JENA OSMAN was born in Philadelphia in 1963. Her book *The Character* won the Barnard New Women Poets Prize in 1998 and was published by Beacon Press in 1999. With Juliana Spahr, she is coeditor of the interdisciplinary arts journal *Chain*. She has received grants from the National Endowment for the Arts, the New York Foundation for the Arts, and the Fund for Poetry. She lives in Philadelphia and teaches at Temple University.

Of "Starred Together," Osman writes: "This poem describes my looking at three works of art that are about hidden (or unseen) populations in New York City: Abigail Child's film *B/side*, Merry Alpern's book of photographs *Dirty Windows*, and a photo-essay by Margaret Morton called 'Pepe Otero: Architect of Shantytown.' It seemed to me that all three investigate the edgy relationship between documentary and aesthetic experiences. As a viewer I found myself seeing these works as beautiful and narrative, yet at the same time the works critiqued that response. They asked me to question beauty—to be conscious of how a desire for a 'transporting' aesthetic experience can lead to the elimination of sight (sites)."

CARL PHILLIPS was born in Everett, Washington, in 1959. He is the author of six books of poems, most recently *Pastoral* (Graywolf, 2000), *The Tether* (2001), and *Rock Harbor* (2002), the last two from Farrar, Straus and Giroux. He received last year's Lambda Literary Award in poetry. He has also won an award in literature from the American Academy of Arts and Letters. Phillips teaches at Washington University in St. Louis.

Of "Fretwork," Phillips writes: "When is enough enough? At that point when we realize that 'what will suffice' not only will, but may have to suffice? The body is restive, or I don't want it. Rough country. *Briar, clover, thorn—all three shall figure.* I woke with more or less those words in my head. Like waking from a mistake better off forgotten. I stayed in bed all morning and wrote the poem. Unexpectedly, a love poem. And a valediction—briefly—to all the struggling against those parts of love that bring with them only peace."

PAM REHM was born in Pennsylvania in 1967. Her books include *Gone to Earth* (Flood Editions, 2001), *To Give It Up* (Sun and Moon Press, 1995), *The Garment in Which No One Had Slept* (Burning Deck, 1993), *Piecework* (o.blek editions, 1992), and *Pollux* (LEAVE Books, 1992). Married with two children, she lives in New York City.

Of "A roof is no guarantee," Rehm writes: "This poem is about the frustration of living in a culture that separates humans from the natural world. It's a poem that wonders what it means to live among things that I wouldn't consider essential to living. The sparrows are a reference to Luke 12:6."

ADRIENNE RICH was born in Baltimore, Maryland, in 1929. She has lived in California since 1984. Her most recent books, all from Norton, are *Midnight Salvage: Poems 1995–98* (1999), *Arts of the Possible: Essays and Conversations* (2000), and *Fox: Poems 1998–2000* (2001). She was the guest editor of *The Best American Poetry 1996*.

Of "Ends of the Earth," Rich writes: "Writing in an artists' residence in New Mexico, in a season of high winds and forest fires, my predecessor in the house, a photographer of extreme landscapes, whom I had and have never met; spectral intimacy of solitude shared with absent presence—the roots of the poem."

CORRINE ROBINS was born in Manhattan and has spent most of her life in that borough. She has lived in SoHo since 1973. Since 1978 she has taught art history at the School of Visual Arts and art criticism at Pratt Institute in Brooklyn. She has written about art since 1966, first for *ARTS Magazine* and later for *Art in America*. Her textbook, *The Pluralist Era: American Art 1968–1981*, was published in 1984 by HarperCollins and as an Icon paperback in 1985. She began writing poetry in 1980. Her first full-length poetry collection, *Marble Goddesses with Technicolor Skins*, was published by Segue Books in 2000. Since 1991 she has coordinated the annual Poets for Choice reading series (a benefit for Planned Parenthood of New York) at the Ceres Gallery in New York City.

Of *"Les Demoiselles d'Avignon,"* Robins writes: "Picasso as a great artist and less as a great man has always fascinated me. In my poems I write about something I don't know (that interests or puzzles me) because by the time it's finished I learn what I didn't know. This poem combines a number of my interests: my love for the painting, my dedication to art history and feminist views, the anger that pumps up the poem. I hope the reader will regard it as confrontational rather than judgmental."

ELIZABETH ROBINSON was born in Denver, Colorado, in 1961. Her books include *Harrow* (Omnidawn Press, 2001) and *House Made of Silver* (Kelsey Street, 2000). Her book *Pure Descent,* a 2001 National Poetry Series winner, will be published by Sun and Moon Press. With Colleen Lookingbill, she coedits Etherdome Press, and is one of five editors of a new magazine, *26*.

Robinson writes: "I had received a brochure in the mail from the Baptist Peace Fellowship. It outlined twelve Baptist principles for peace and justice, each accompanied by supporting biblical references. I began writing 'Tenets of Roots and Trouble' as a kind of response to this document. I was interested in the historical disconnect between the biblical narratives and the application of them to present political and military concerns. I was also captivated by the local, concrete imagery of the biblical references and I wanted to co-opt them for my own poem. So this piece is partially a disruption of the received language of the Bible and the brochure, and partially my own struggling hermeneutic."

IRA SADOFF was born in Brooklyn, New York, in 1945. He is the author of six collections of poems, most recently *Grazing* (University of Illionis Press, 1998), which won the Jerome Shestack Prize from *American Poetry Review.* He has also written a novel and *The Ira Sadoff Reader.* He has been awarded grants from the National Endowment for the Arts and the John Simon Guggenheim Foundation and is currently the Dana Professor of Poetry at Colby College in Maine.

Of "Self-Portrait with Critic," Sadoff writes: "Poets with half a brain never respond to reviews, especially dumb reviews in very small magazines. But I found myself engaged by one reviewer's unmitigated rage. She confused biography with lyric speakers and constantly misread tone and subjects. That sparked the poem. What surprised me was that by middle-drafts I'd found myself identifying with the reviewer. How many times had I misread people the way the reviewer had misread me? Experience had told me over and over that identity was a needy fiction. We have no *essence.* I'd forgotten how subjectivity and our rich contradictions make us elusive and ineffable. My own history—no less the history of others—with its struggles and frailties, often remained repressed, barely visible or out of reach.

" 'Self-Portrait' took months to write. There were so many gaps, distortions, and blind spots. I experienced this instability with every line I wrote: every time a line moved toward meaning it reduced experience. I originally wanted the poem to be a densely layered self-portrait like a Modigliani, where surfaces are built with layer after layer of paint. Thus the jagged syntax, the turns in the poem, the working toward and away from resolution. I'm grateful to the reviewer for reminding me how our projections and histories obscure and mangle the way we see the world."

HUGH SEIDMAN was born in Brooklyn in 1940. His poetry has won two New York State poetry grants and three National Endowment for the Arts fellowships. His first book, *Collecting Evidence* (Yale University Press, 1970), won the Yale Series of Younger Poets Prize. He has taught writing at the University of Wisconsin, Yale University, Columbia University, and the New School University. His *Selected Poems: 1965–1995* was published by Miami University Press in 1995. A chapbook of the poem "12 Views of Freetown, 1 View of Bumbuna" was published by Half Moon Bay Press in 2002.

Of "I Do Not Know Myself," Seidman writes: "Walking home from work on Hudson past Morton toward Bethune. Summer, early evening. Thinking of S's anger and lust for liberation. Of Buddha's *suffering as desire* (craving and attachment). Of Jung's *none can illuminate all the darkness.* Also:

"Dogen, who later brought Soto Zen to Japan, sought the depths of Buddhism in China. He visited many temples, but still was unsatisfied. One day he observed a very old monk drying mushrooms in the hot sun.

" 'Why do you kneel doing the job of a junior monk, when you are a senior monk of the temple?' asked Dogen.

" 'If I do not do this, if I do not work here and now, who could understand? I am not you; I am not others. Others are not me. Others cannot have the experience. I must dry these mushrooms, today, at this moment. Go away, so I may work!'

"Dogen was startled and experienced *satori* (enlightenment)."

—from *Karate: Technique and Spirit* by T. Nakamura, Grand Master, Seido Karate

REGINALD SHEPHERD was born in New York City in 1963. He was raised in tenements and housing projects in the Bronx. He received his B.A. from Bennington College and MFA degrees from Brown University and the University of Iowa. His first book, *Some Are Drowning,* was published by the University of Pittsburgh Press in 1994 as winner of the Associated Writing Programs' Award in Poetry. Pittsburgh published his second book, *Angel, Interrupted,* in 1996, and his third book, *Wrong,* in 1999. His fourth book, *Otherhood,* is forthcoming from Pittsburgh. He has taught at Northern Illinois University and Cornell University and currently lives in Florida, where magnolias (and oaks) are evergreens and it doesn't snow.

Shepherd writes: " 'You Also, Nightingale' was originally intended to be part of a series of poems deploying the figure of Petrarch in various incongruous contexts that would all nonetheless incorporate notions and notations of song, as well as various images of the laurel. I'm very good at coming up with projects, but very bad at following through on them. I completed one other poem to which 'You Also, Nightingale' is a kind of pendant; entitled 'Refrain,' it was published in *Indiana Review.* I planned another poem that would juxtapose Petrarch and Osiris, but during the course of composition Osiris took it over and Petrarch wandered away; it was out of the scraps he left behind that I wrote 'You Also, Nightingale.' I realize in rereading the poem that the image of Petrarch singing with his back turned to me echoes that of Eliot's mermaids singing only to each other. It's a version of my relation to the Western literary tradition: I listen to the singing but it's not meant for me. The poem is my attempt to make it mine, but the music can run you over if you're not careful. Forsythia and magnolia blossom at the very onset of spring, well before the other flowering trees and shrubs; magnolia and laurel are, of course, close relatives. I've always believed in being accurate when I can.

"The poem's title is an homage to MacLeish's 'You, Andrew Marvell' and his 'You Also, Gaius Valerius Catullus,' for no other reason than that his titles address poets and mine speaks of one; the nightingale belongs, of course, to Keats. Poetry and high finance are among the few realms in which theft is rewarded. I also liked the implication of 'Hey you, bird, I'm talking to you.' "

RON SILLIMAN was born in Pasco, Washington, in 1946. He grew up in the Berkeley area of California. Since 1995, he has lived with his wife and two sons in Chester County, Pennsylvania, where he works as a market analyst in the computer industry. The winner of the 1985 Poetry Center Book Award for his prose poem *Paradise,* Silliman was a 1998–99 Pew Fellow in the Arts and has twice received grants from the California Arts Council. His anthology, *In the American Tree* (National Poetry Foundation, second edition, 2001), continues in print and his collection of talks and essays, *The New Sentence* (Roof, 1987), has gone through multiple printings. Since 1979, Silliman has been writing a poem entitled *The Alphabet*. Volumes published thus far from that project include *ABC* (Tuumba Press, 1983), *Demo to Ink* (Chax Press, 1992), *Jones* (Generator Press, 1993), *Lit* (Potes & Poets Press, 1987), *Manifest* (Zasterle Press, 1990), *N/O* (Roof Press, 1994), *Paradise* (Burning Deck, 1985), ® (Drogue Press, 1999), *Toner* (Potes & Potes Press, 1992), *What* (The Figures, 1988), and *Xing* (Meow Press, 1996). Salt will reissue his long poem *Tjanting* in 2002.

Of "For Larry Eigner, *Silent*," Silliman writes: "Larry Eigner was one of the great poets of my parents' generation, and a most generous friend. Because of cerebral palsy, he was confined to a wheelchair and lived an extraordinary life within strict physical limitations. I had moved to Pennsylvania just a few months before he died, and his passing was my first real act of grieving for all that I'd left behind."

DALE SMITH was born in Garland, Texas, in 1967. Thorp Springs Press published his book *American Rambler* (2000). A daybook, *The Flood and the Garden*, was recently published by First Intensity. Both are available through Small Press Distribution in Berkeley, California. He has lived in Yemen, Oregon, and California, and currently resides in Austin with his wife, the poet Hoa Nguyen. Together they edit *Skanky Possum*, a newsletter of poetry and poetics.

Of "Poem after Haniel Long," Smith writes: "My poem comes from a digressive narrative, *American Rambler*, that considers in prose and verse the extraordinary peregrinations of the conquistador-turned-healer Alvar Nuñez Cabeza de Vaca. He drifted on a barge across the Gulf of Mexico from Florida, landing near Galveston, Texas, in November 1527. Of the five hundred men in his expedition only four survived. His was an inversion of the standard model of conquest, and his narrative of the nine years it took for him to return to Spain provides a humbled experience of the New World so very different from the earlier conquest in Mexico of Hernán Cortés.

"Teacher and poet Haniel Long (1888–1956) wrote a prose retelling of Cabeza de Vaca's spiritual trials in the New World. His *Interlinear to Cabeza de Vaca* reads into the official accounts to retrieve the impacted, spiritual roots to that experience. Long evokes in spare language the depths of suffering, encounters with native peoples, and extraordinary animistic experience of the archaic conditions to which Cabeza de Vaca submitted. He shows a tremendous complexity of geographic and spiritual encounter, the pressures of survival in conflict with the motivations and cultural values of imperialist Spain.

"My poem borrows generously from that great writer's work. It was written to acknowledge and pay tribute to the attentive care delivered in his *Interlinear*. He is one of few writers to retrieve an experience of the New World as psychic, or spiritual, conflict, rather than the socioeconomic enterprise it became."

GUSTAF SOBIN was born in Boston in 1935 and attended the Choate School and Brown University, from which he graduated in 1958. In 1962 he moved to southern France, where he has lived, written, taught, and translated ever since. His books of poetry are *Wind Chysalid's Rattle* (Montemora, 1980), *Celebration of the Sound Through* (Montemora, 1982), *The Earth as Air* (New Directions, 1985), *Voyaging Portraits* (New Directions, 1988), *Breaths' Burials* (New Directions, 1995), *By the Bias of Sound* (Talisman House, 1995), *Towards the Blanched Alphabets* (Talisman House, 1998), and *In the Name of the Neither* (Talisman House, 2002). His novels include *Venus Blue* (Little, Brown, 1992), *Dark Mirrors* (Bloomsbury, 1992), *The Fly-Truffler* (W. W. Norton, 2000), and *In Pursuit of a Vanishing Star* (W. W. Norton, 2002). A book of essays entitled *Luminous Debris: Reflecting on Vestige in Provence and Languedoc* was published by the University of California Press in 2000.

Sobin writes: "'In Way of Introduction,' like much of my poetry, reflects upon language—as vectorial agent—to reach past itself in an attempt to touch upon that hallucinatory field in which cognition first originated. There, that is, where speech becomes virtually speechless, where the verb comes free of its quantitative mission, a plentitude awaits the receptive. Mystics such as Meister Eckhart have spoken of that dimension as *Daz niht:* that nothing out of which all things emanate. Lovers, *illuminés,* individuals exposed to extreme life-threatening conditions, have experienced similar epiphanies. Even in an age such as ours characterized by redundancy, by the remorseless beat of one referent against another, there remains a level of discourse in which the word unwritten, unspoken, divested of its very properties, tends—under certain circumstances—to substantiate."

JULIANA SPAHR was born in Chillicothe, Ohio, in 1966. She has worked as a country-and-western disc jockey, as a parking lot attendant, as a bartender, and many times as a secretary. She currently teaches at the

University of Hawaii at Manoa. Her books include *Fuck You-Aloha-I Love You* (Wesleyan University Press, 2001), *Everybody's Autonomy: Connective Reading and Collective Identity* (University of Alabama Press, 2001), and *Response* (Sun and Moon Press, 1996). She coedits the journal *Chain* with Jena Osman (archive at http://www.temple.edu/chain). She frequently self-publishes her work. Eventually an online version of this work will be available at http://epc.buffalo.edu/authors/spahr.

Of "Some of We and the Land That Was Never Ours," Spahr writes: "We were tourists. There were long lines. My mother waited in them. I sat outside and took notes. In the park, someone was singing we are all in this world together. There were some grapes. Someone was feeding sparrows, making them perch on the thumb and eat out of the hand if they wanted any food. The sparrows preferred to eat on the ground. I was thinking about a story I had heard about a French grandfather who left early in my father's life, moved to Canada, and died by falling off a horse. I thought about the vines that grew in France, then came as cuttings to California, then went back to France after a blight. I thought about who owned what. And divisions. And songs sung in bars. And inaugural poems. I was just trying to figure out this day and how things came together. I came home and used a translation machine (http://babel. altavista.com) to push my notes back and forth between French and English until a new sort of English came out, this poem."

JOHN TAGGART was born in Perry, Iowa, in 1942. He was educated at Earlham College, the University of Chicago, and Syracuse University. He recently retired from Shippensburg University (Pennsylvania), where he taught literature. During the 1960s and '70s he edited the poetry magazine *Maps*. He is currently interested in gardening—specifically, the planting of trees. He has published nine volumes of poetry, the most recent of which is *When the Saints* (Talisman House, 1999). He has also published a collection of essays on contemporary poetry and poetics, *Songs of Degrees* (University of Alabama Press, 1994), and a book on the painter Edward Hopper, *Remaining in Light* (SUNY Press, 1993).

Of "Call," Taggart writes: "I write without internal punctuation because I want to bring the reader into a greater intimacy with the poem, i.e., not to read with the cool scanning eye only, but also with the reader's voice, with at least some movement of the reader's lips. There's some irony about that in the poem. For what reading enunciates there is silence, not merely dead sound or the cancellation of sound, but rather a moment containing everything we mean by the words 'sympathy' or 'care.' So a moment in a telephone conversation in which everything was stated, and nothing in fact was said. It's startling, even shocking, to be cared for. Perhaps even more so when, after a lapse of some time, the realization comes 'out of the blue' that one has, indeed, been cared for. Also humbling, beyond any deserving."

SAM TRUITT was born in Washington, DC, in 1960. He is a graduate of Kenyon College and Brown University, where he received an MFA. He is the author of *Anamorphosis Eisenhower* (Lost Roads Publishers, 1998) and of *Vertical Elegies 1* (Ugly Duckling Presse). He performs works of magnitude poetry regularly in the Loudmouth Collective's bimonthly Anti-Reading series in New York City, where he lives and works.

Of "from *Raton Rex, Part 1,*" Truitt writes: "In the summer of 1996 my friend Tom Donnelly, the redoubtable Australian vet, turned forty. For his birthday, I thought to write a book by composing forty lines each day for forty days, which I more or less did. I chose a short line because I was curious to concentrate on the tumbling, energetic enjambments this made possible—and also because it would make it easier to meet my commitment. *Raton Rex* is pretty much what happened, or what was occurring to me, both eventfully and thoughtfully, in my life in New York. I think it was also informed by something of the sense that writing poetry is a bit like trimming the toenails of a corpse.

"*Raton Rex* means 'rat king' in Latin. A rat king is a mysterious rat-nest phenomenon in which Tom was interested. It occurs when rats are packed too close in and a group of sometimes as many as thirty-two, presumably writhing together, get their tails entangled and Gordian knotted. Unable to get free, they die of thirst—although it is also true that sometimes, unselfishly, their unstuck brethren feed them for life. The term may derive from an early belief that the rats thus tail-locked were one organism, a supreme rat with many bodies."

JEAN VALENTINE was born in 1934 in Chicago. She is the author of eight books of poetry, most recently *The Cradle of the Real Life* (Wesleyan, 2000). She lives and works in New York City.

Of "Do flies remember us," Valentine writes: "My friend the poet Julie Carr made this poem better (by suggesting I take some of it out). I'm happy Don Revell, and now Robert Creeley, have printed it."

LEWIS WARSH was born in New York City in 1944. He is the author of more than twenty-five books of poetry, fiction, and autobiography.

Recent publications include a book of poems, *The Origin of the World* (Creative Arts, 2001), a book of stories, *Touch of the Whip* (Singing Horse, 2001), a novel, *Ted's Favorite Skirt* (Spuyten Duyvil, 2002), a collaboration with Julie Harrison, *Debtor's Prison* (Granary Books, 2001), and *The Angel Hair Anthology* (Granary Books, 2001), coedited with Anne Waldman. He has taught at the Poetry Project, Naropa University, SUNY Albany, the New School, and is now on the faculty of Long Island University in Brooklyn. He is editor and publisher of United Artists Books.

Warsh writes: " 'Eye Contact' is one of a series of poems I wrote during the 1990s. I wanted a form where I could include everything—different voices, narratives, memories, anecdotes, headlines, misinformation. Everything that ever happened to anyone down through time. Composing this poem involved accumulating lines (or fragments) and then arranging them. Sometimes I discarded lines that didn't seem to fit— though often I would use these lines in another poem where they made more sense. I wanted to create a feeling that was ongoing, like life itself, with no beginning or end, more like a spiral into the unknown than a straight line leading somewhere familiar. I never knew what the poem would be about other than itself until I reached a kind of midway point and then I realized that I wanted it to be about, say, the Korean woman in the store on the corner—and that would take over. The lines are like lines of poetry but they're also sentences, statements, propositions. I've always written poetry and fiction simultaneously—this feels like a synthesis of the two."

CLAIRE NICOLAS WHITE, born in the Netherlands in 1925, came to New York in 1940 and attended the French Lycée and Smith College. She has lived on Long Island since 1947, except for four years at the American Academy in Rome, where her husband was in residence. She is the author of a novel, *The Death of the Orange Trees* (Doubleday, 1963); a memoir, *Fragments of Stained Glass* (Mercury House, 1989); a book of poetry, *Biography and Other Poems* (Doubleday, 1981); and four chapbooks. She has translated three novels from the Dutch—*The Assault*, by Harry Mulisch; *The Vanishing*, by Tim Krabbe; and *My Father's War*, by Adriaan van Dis—as well as poetry from the French and the Dutch. She teaches at the Walt Whitman Birthplace and writes art reviews.

Of "Return to Saint Odilienberg, Easter 2000," White writes: "The church of Saint Odilienberg was first built in the eighth century, destroyed during World War II, and beautifully restored in the 1950s. My father, a stained-glass painter, returned to Holland after the war to make all the windows, and my mother, a sculptress, did the Stations of the Cross. It was my father's favorite church and he asked to be buried there, near the town of Roermond, where he was born.

"I brought my grandchildren to this small village in the south of Holland. The Easter service was perfectly sung in Gregorian chant, and a village orchestra performed Handel's 'Hallelujah.' "

NATHAN WHITING was born in Urbana, Illinois, in 1946 and moved to New York City in 1968. The author of eight books of poetry, he ran more than seventy-five races of fifty miles or longer but has more recently taken up dance, performing with Sara Pearson, Douglas Dunn, J. Mandle Performance, Bhuto dancer Min Tanaka, and many others. He has also presented his own choreography.

Whiting writes: "As a dancer over fifty, I believe it is important to observe the detailed movements of people and the various ways they express themselves as they exist through the world. 'In Charge' is the poetic equivalent of a short character dance, both the listening and the imagination. Still an outdoors person, I find the city a wonderful presenter of the human theater, a place where self-consciousness loses itself among crowds and the remnants of human dignity often appear with surprising clarity."

DARA WIER was born in New Orleans, Louisiana, in 1949. Her eight collections of poetry include *Hat on a Pond* (Verse Press, 2002), *Voyages in English* (Carnegie Mellon, 2001), and *Our Master Plan* (Carnegie Mellon, 1997). The Guggenheim Foundation, the National Endowment for the Arts, and the Massachusetts Cultural Council have supported her work with fellowships. In 2001 *The American Poetry Review* awarded a selection of her poems the Jerome J. Shestack Poetry Prize and *Voyages in English* was one of five finalists for the Phi Beta Kappa Book Award. She lives in Amherst, Massachusetts, where she teaches in the program for poets and writers at the University of Massachusetts.

Wier writes: "In 'Illumined with the Light of Fitfully Burning Censers' the woman keeps finding a good parking place but continues searching for same throughout her neighborhood on, say, a telemonitor, in wanted posters, in the faces of strangers or near-strangers. I felt kindly toward her going about her job as she did. I didn't know what she was thinking when she, for instance, looked at wanted posters. That seemed spooky: I didn't think I could say what was on her mind."

CHARLES WRIGHT was born in Pickwick Dam, Tennessee, in 1935. He teaches at the University of Virginia in Charlottesville. His most recent books are *Negative Blue: Selected Later Poems* (2000) and *A Short History of the Shadow* (2002), both from Farrar, Straus and Giroux. In 1952 he started and played every game for the Christ School Green Wave baseball team and went hitless (0–1952) until the last game of the season, when he doubled in the winning run against Asheville High School. "Needless to say," he notes, "our pitcher was throwing some real heat."

Of "Nostalgia II," Wright writes: "The poem is pretty much its own commentary. Memories of my beginnings (at age twenty-three) as a *poetista*, with my old friend Harold Schimmel (now an Israeli poet), both of us U.S. Army members in Verona, Italy. Great times—the lira at 621 to a dollar as God intended, everything new and undiminished. Harold and I had an early passion for Pound, who wrote about our town (Verona), and whose books were printed there. Italy stunned me into poetry. Everyone has his secret drawer. This was mine."

JOHN YAU was born in Lynn, Massachusetts, in 1950, shortly after his parents left Shanghai. He received a B.A. from Bard College and an MFA from Brooklyn College. He is critic in residence at the Mount Royal Graduate School (Maryland Institute College of Art) and on the faculty of the Avery Graduate School (Bard College). He has published more than a dozen volumes of poetry, fiction, and criticism. His most recent books include a collaboration with the artist Archie Rand, *100 More Jokes from the Book of the Dead* (Meritage Press, 2000), *My Heart Is That Eternal Rose Tattoo* (Black Sparrow Press, 2000), and *Borrowed Love Poems* (Penguin Putnam, 2001). He lives in Manhattan.

Yau writes: "In early Renaissance paintings the outside (or world) and inside (or interior space) are often collapsed together, or so it seems. The poem 'A Sheaf of Pleasant Voices' started with that recognition, which I then tried both to expand upon and subvert. Not one voice, then, but more than one. As with many poems I (whoever that is) write (do I write them?), I want the line, stanza, and word-next-to-word placement to go in unexpected directions (think of Jackson Pollock), to break off and begin elsewhere. Finally, I was also reconsidering Stéphane Mallarmé's belief that the world exists to end up in a book. This seems a rather safe possibility next to its opposite, that what is contained within a book exists to end up in the world. This is where the poem took me, and where it left me."

MAGAZINES WHERE THE POEMS
WERE FIRST PUBLISHED

AGNI, ed. Askold Melnyczuk. Boston University, 236 Bay State Road, Boston, MA 02215.

American Poetry Review, eds. Stephen Berg, David Bonanno, and Arthur Vogelsgang. 1721 Walnut Street, Philadelphia, PA 19103.

The Antioch Review, poetry ed. Judith Hall. P.O. Box 148, Yellow Springs, OH 45387.

Barrow Street, eds. Patricia Carlin, Peter Covino, Lois Hirschkowitz, and Melissa Hotchkiss. P.O. Box 2017, Old Chelsea Station, New York, NY 10113.

Beloit Poetry Journal, ed. Marion K. Stocking. 24 Berry Cove Road, Lamoine, ME 04605.

Bombay Gin. Writing and Poetics Dept., Naropa University, 2130 Arapahoe Avenue, Boulder, CO 80302.

Boondoggle, ed. Eric Malone. 80 Silver Lane, Sunderland, MA 01375.

Boston Review, poetry eds. Mary Jo Bang and Timothy Donnelly. E53-407, MIT, 30 Wadsworth Street, Cambridge, MA 02139-4307.

The Café Review, ed. Steve Luttrell. c/o Yes Books, 20 Danforth Street, Portland, ME 04101.

Can We Have Our Ball Back?, ed. Jim Behrle. http://canwehaveourballback.com/

Chicago Review, poetry ed. Eric Elshtain. 5801 South Kenwood Avenue, Chicago, IL 60637.

Colorado Review, poetry eds. Jorie Graham and Donald Revell. Dept. of English, Colorado State University, Ft. Collins, CO 80523.

Connecticut Review, ed. Vivian Shipley. Dept. of English, Southern Connecticut State University, New Haven, CT 06515.

Crux, ed. William.E. Reuben. P.O. Box 255, South Londonderry, VT 05155.

Deluxe Rubber Chicken, ed. Mark Peters. http://wings.buffalo.edu/epc/ezines deluxe/

Facture, eds. Lindsay Hill and Paul Naylor. P.O. Box 337, Cedar Ridge, CA 95924.

Hambone, ed. Nathaniel Mackey. 134 Humbolt Street, Santa Cruz, CA 95060.

Hanging Loose, eds. Robert Hershon, Dick Lourie, Mark Pawlak, and Ron Schreiber. 231 Wyckoff Street, Brooklyn, NY 11217.

Harvard Review, poetry ed. Daniel Bosch. Lamont Library, Harvard University, Cambridge, MA 02138.

The Hat, eds. Jordan Davis and Chris Edgar. 331 East 9th Street #1, New York, NY 10003.

Jacket, ed. Jonathan Tranter. http://www.jacket.zip.com.au/

jubilat, eds. Robert N. Casper, Christian Howkey, Kelly LeFave, and Michael Teig. Dept. of English, 482 Bartlett Hall, University of Massachusetts, Amherst, MA 01003-0510.

The Kenyon Review, ed. David Lynn. Kenyon College, Gambier, OH 43022.

Mungo vs. Ranger, eds. Roger Snell and Jeremiah McNichols. 632 Lyon Street, San Francisco, CA 94117.

New American Writing, eds. Paul Hoover and Maxine Chernoff. 369 Molino Avenue, Mill Valley, CA 94941.

New England Review, poetry ed. C. Dale Young. Middlebury College, Middlebury, VT 05753.

The New York Review of Books, eds. Robert B. Silvers and Barbara Epstein. 1755 Broadway, 5th Floor, New York, NY 10019.

The New Yorker, poetry ed. Alice Quinn. 4 Times Square, New York, NY 10036.

Pleiades, poetry ed. Kevin Prufer. Dept. of English, Central Missouri State University, Warrensburg, MO 64093.

Pharos, c/o The British Institute, 11, rue de Constantine, Paris 75007, France.

Ploughshares, poetry ed. David Daniel. Emerson College, 100 Beacon Street, Boston, MA 02116.

Poetry, ed. Joseph Parisi. 60 W. Walton Street, Chicago, IL 60610-3380.

Pressed Wafer, ed. William Corbett. 9 Columbus Square, Boston, MA 02116.

Seneca Review, ed. Deborah Tall. Hobart and William Smith Colleges, Geneva, NY 14456-3397.

Skanky Possum, eds. Dale Smith and Hoa Nguyen. 2925 Higgins Street, Austin TX 78722-1408.

Slate, poetry ed. Robert Pinsky. http://www.slate.com/

Slope, ed. Ethan Paquin. http://www.slope.org/

Talisman: A Journal of Contemporary Poetry and Poetics. Eds. Joseph Donahue and Edward Foster. P.O. Box 3157, Jersey City, NJ 07303-3157.

3rd Bed, poetry ed. Hermine Meinhard. 17 Union Avenue, Jamaica Plain, MA 02130.

The Threepenny Review, poetry ed. Wendy Lesser. P.O. Box 9131, Berkeley, CA 94709.

Verse, eds. Brian Henry and Andrew Zawacki. English Department, Plymouth State College, Plymouth, NH 03264.

Volt, ed. Gillian Conoley. P.O. Box 657, Corte Madera, CA 94976-0657.

Witness, ed. Peter Stine. Oakland Community College, 27055 Orchard Lake Road, Farmington Hills, MI 48334.

ACKNOWLEDGMENTS

The series editor thanks Mark Bibbins for his invaluable assistance. Thanks go also to Gillian Blake, Rachel Sussman, M. K. Laughlin, Erich Hobbing, and Jay Schweitzer of Scribner and to Glen Hartley and Lynn Chu of Writers' Representatives.

Grateful acknowledgment is made of the magazines in which these poems first appeared and the magazine editors who selected them. Unless otherwise noted, copyright to the poems is held by the individual poets.

Rae Armantrout: "Up to Speed" appeared in *Chicago Review*. Reprinted by permission of the poet.

John Ashbery: "The Pearl Fishers" from *Your Name Here*. Copyright © 2000 by John Ashbery. Reprinted by permission of the poet and Farrar, Straus and Giroux. First appeared in *Verse*.

Amiri Baraka: "The Golgotha Local" appeared in *Skanky Possum*. Reprinted by permission of the poet.

Charles Bernstein: "12²" appeared in *Slope*. Reprinted by permission of the poet.

Anselm Berrigan: "from *Zero Star Hotel*" appeared in *Bombay Gin*. Reprinted by permission of the poet.

Frank Bidart: "Injunction" appeared in *Ploughshares*. Reprinted by permission of the poet.

Jenny Boully: "The Body" from *The Body*. Copyright © 2002 by Jenny Boully. Reprinted by permission of the poet and Slope Editions. First appeared in *Seneca Review*.

T. Alan Broughton: "Ballad of the Comely Woman" appeared in *Beloit Poetry Journal*. Reprinted by permission of the poet.

Michael Burkard: "What I Threw into the Grave" appeared in *Pennsylvania Collection Agency*. Copyright © 2001 by Michael Burkard. Reprinted by permission of the poet and New Issues Press. First appeared in *jubilat*.

Anne Carson: "Opposed Glimpse of Alice James, Garth James, Henry James, Robertson James and William James" appeared in *The Threepenny Review*. Reprinted by permission of the poet.

Elizabeth Biller Chapman: "On the Screened Porch" appeared in *Poetry*. Reprinted by permission of the poet and the editor of *Poetry*.

Tom Clark: "Lullaby for Cuckoo" appeared in *Skanky Possum*. Reprinted by permission of the poet.

Peter Cooley: "Corpus Delicti" appeared in *Pleiades*. Reprinted by permission of the poet.

Clark Coolidge: "Traced Red Dot" appeared in *New American Writing* and *Jacket*. Reprinted by permission of the poet.

Joseph Lease: " 'Broken World' (For James Assatly)" appeared in *Colorado Review*. Reprinted by permission of the poet.

Timothy Liu: "Felix Culpa" appeared in *Ploughshares*. Reprinted by permission of the poet.

Nathaniel Mackey: "On Antiphon Island" appeared in *jubilat*. Reprinted by permission of the poet.

Jackson Mac Low: "And Even You Elephants? (Stein 139/Titles 35)" appeared in *Deluxe Rubber Chicken*. Reprinted by permission of the poet.

Steve Malmude: "Perfect Front Door" appeared in *The Hat*. Reprinted by permission of the poet.

Sarah Manguso: "Address to Winnie in Paris" from *The Captain Lands in Paradise*. Copyright © 2002 by Sarah Manguso. Reprinted by permission of the poet and Alice James Books. First appeared in *jubilat*.

Harry Mathews: "Butter & Eggs" appeared in *Boston Review*. Reprinted by permission of the poet.

Duncan McNaughton: "The quarry (1–13)" appeared in *Hambone*. Reprinted by permission of the poet.

W. S. Merwin: "To My Father's Houses" appeared in *The New York Review of Books*. Reprinted by permission of the poet.

Philip Metres: "Ashberries: Letters" appeared in *New England Review*. Reprinted by permission of the poet.

Mộng-Lan: "Trail" appeared in *jubilat*. Reprinted by permission of the poet.

Jennifer Moxley: "Behind the Orbits" appeared in *Pressed Wafer*. Reprinted by permission of the poet.

Eileen Myles: "Sympathy" from *Skies*. Copyright © 2001 by Eileen Myles. Reprinted by permission of the poet and Black Sparrow Press. First appeared in *American Poetry Review*.

Maggie Nelson: "Sunday Night" from *Shiner*. Copyright © 2001 by Maggie Nelson. Reprinted by permission of the poet and Hanging Loose Press. First appeared in *The Hat*.

Charles North: "Sonnet" appeared in *Boston Review*. Reprinted by permission of the poet.

Alice Notley: "Haunt" appeared in *Pharos*. Reprinted by permission of the poet.

D. Nurkse: "Snapshot from Niagara" from *The Rules of Paradise*. Copyright © 2001 by D. Nurkse. Reprinted by permission of the poet and Four Way Books. First appeared in *Barrow Street*.

Sharon Olds: "Frontis Nulla Fides" appeared in *Ploughshares*. Reprinted by permission of the poet.

George Oppen: "Twenty-six Fragments" appeared in *Facture*. Reprinted by permission of Linda Oppen.

Jena Osman: "Starred Together" appeared in *Hambone*. Reprinted by permission of the poet.

Carl Phillips: "Fretwork" appeared in *The Threepenny Review*. Reprinted by permission of the poet.

Pam Rehm: " 'A roof is no guarantee . . .' " from *Gone to Earth*. Copyright © 2001 by Pam Rehm. Reprinted by permission of the poet and Flood Editions. First appeared in *Chicago Review*.